GRAPHIC BIOGRAPHIES

AMELIA EARHART
LEGENDARY AVIATOR

by Jameson Anderson
illustrated by Rod Whigham and
Charles Barnett III

Consultant:
Sammie Morris, Archivist
The George Palmer Putnam Collection of
Amelia Earhart Papers
Purdue University

Capstone press

Mankato, Minnesota

Graphic Library is published by Capstone Press,
1710 Roe Crest Drive, North Mankato, Minnesota 56003.
www.capstonepub.com

Library of Congress Cataloging-in-Publication Data
Anderson, Jameson.
Amelia Earhart: legendary aviator / by Jameson Anderson; illustrated by Rod Whigham and Charles Barnett III.
p. cm.—(Graphic library. Graphic biographies)
Includes bibliographical references and index.
ISBN: 978-0-7368-6496-1 (hardcover)
ISBN: 978-0-7368-9659-7 (softcover pbk.)
1. Earhart, Amelia, 1897–1937—Juvenile literature. 2. Air pilots—United States—Biography—Juvenile literature. 3. Women air pilots—United States—Biography—Juvenile literature. I. Whigham, Rod, 1954– II. Barnett, Charles, III. III. Title. IV. Series.
TL540.E3A75 2007
629.13092—dc22 2006004135

Summary: In graphic novel format, tells the story of Amelia Earhart, the daring female aviator who disappeared while attempting to become the first woman to pilot a plane around the world.

Art Direction and Design
Bob Lentz

Production Artist
Rana Raeuchle

Colorist
Matt Webb

Editor
Christine Peterson

Editor's note: Direct quotations from primary sources are indicated by a yellow background.

Direct quotations appear on the following pages:
Page 17, from a 1928 *New York Times* article written by Amelia Earhart, as published in *East to the Dawn: The Life of Amelia Earhart* by Susan Butler (Reading, Mass.: Addison-Wesley, 1997).
Pages 26 and 27, from the July 2, 1937, radio logs of the U.S. Coast Guard ship *Itasca* as transcribed by The International Group for Historic Aircraft Recovery (TIGHAR) (http://www.tighar.org/Projects/Earhart/Bulletins/37_ItascaLogs/Itascalog.html).

Printed in the United States 5019

TABLE
of
Contents

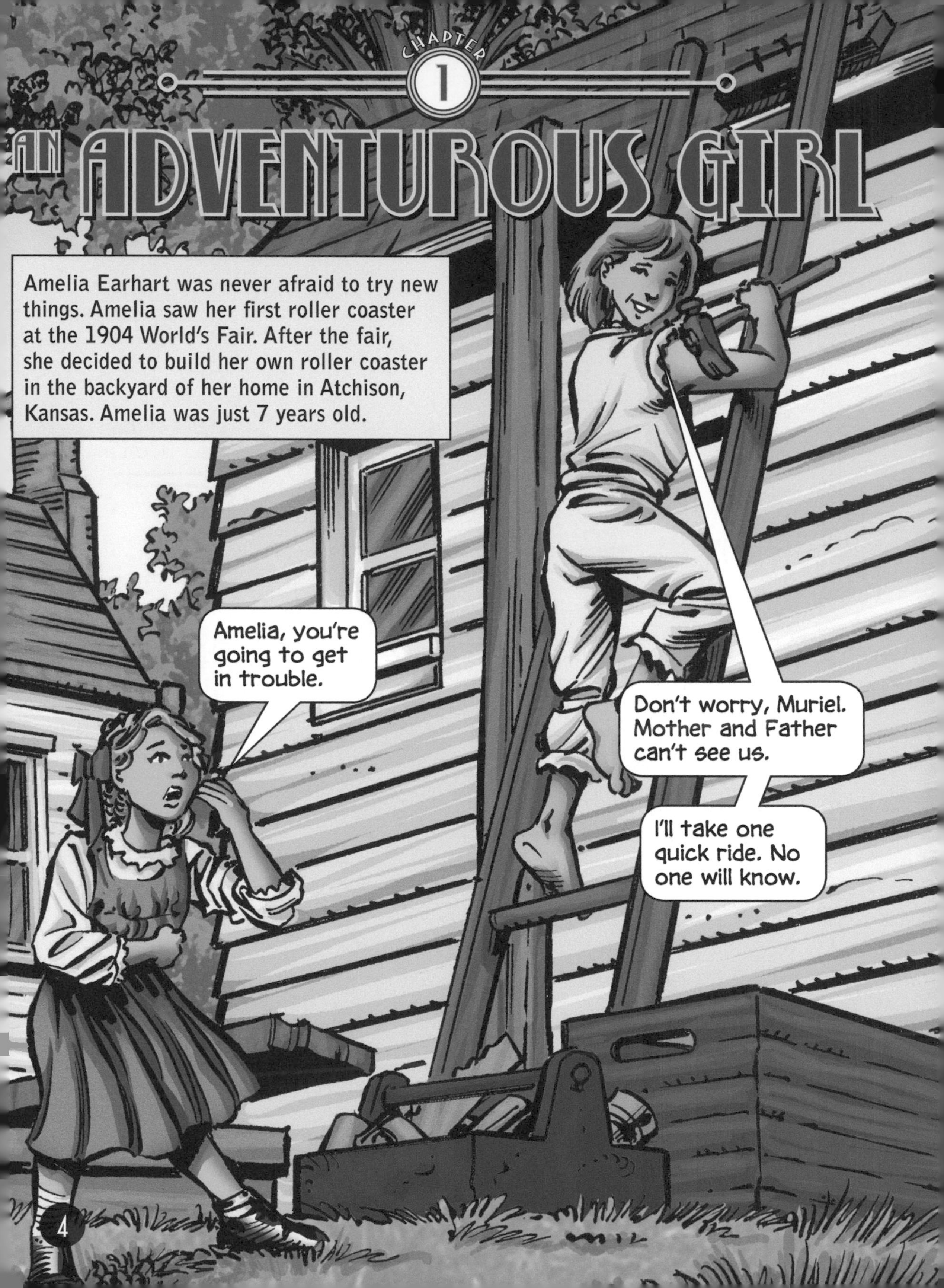
CHAPTER 1
AN ADVENTUROUS GIRL
Amelia Earhart was never afraid to try new things. Amelia saw her first roller coaster at the 1904 World's Fair. After the fair, she decided to build her own roller coaster in the backyard of her home in Atchison, Kansas. Amelia was just 7 years old.
Amelia, you're going to get in trouble.
Don't worry, Muriel. Mother and Father can't see us.
I'll take one quick ride. No one will know.

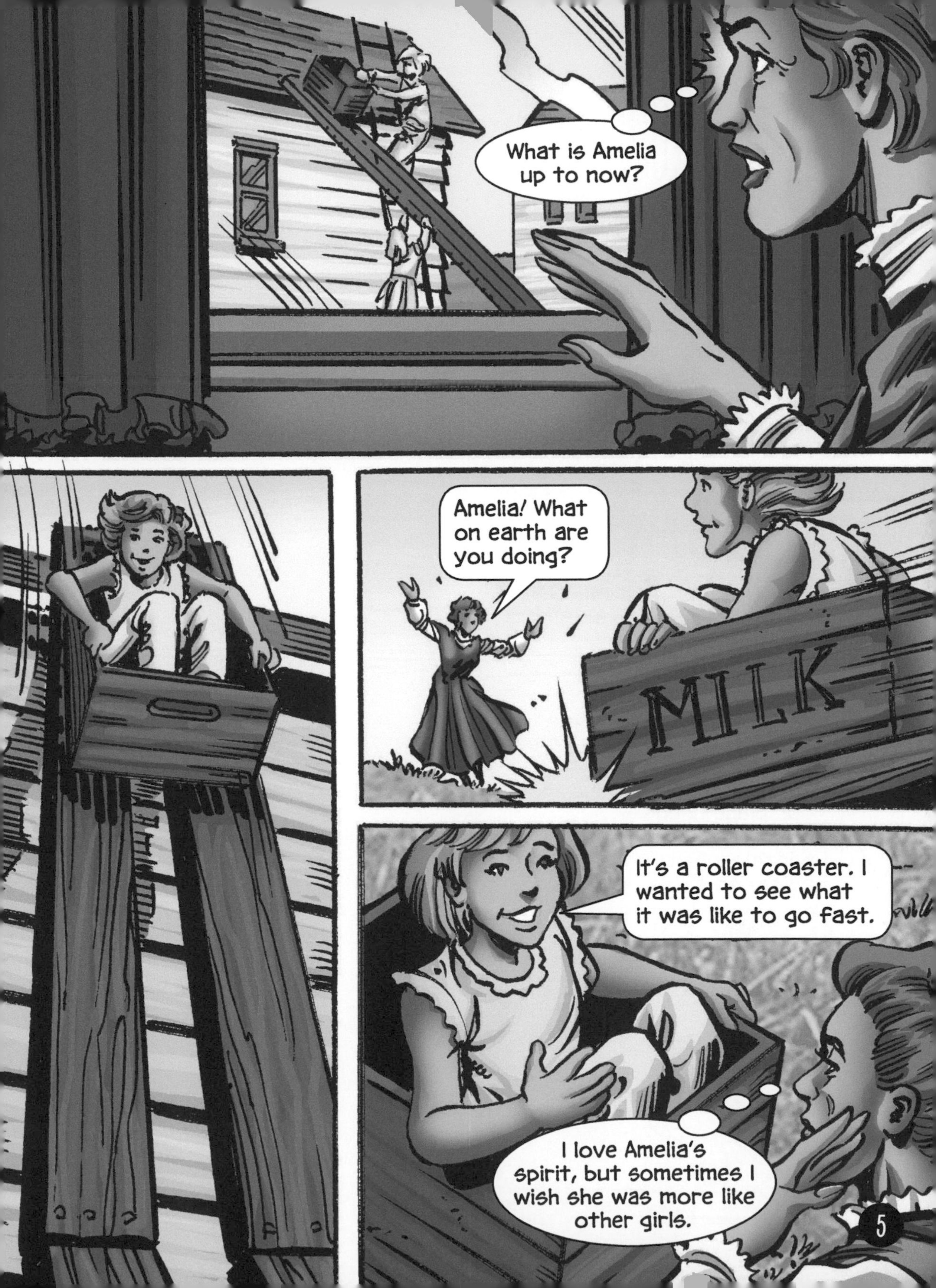
What is Amelia up to now?
Amelia! What on earth are you doing?
MILK
It's a roller coaster. I wanted to see what it was like to go fast.
I love Amelia's spirit, but sometimes I wish she was more like other girls.

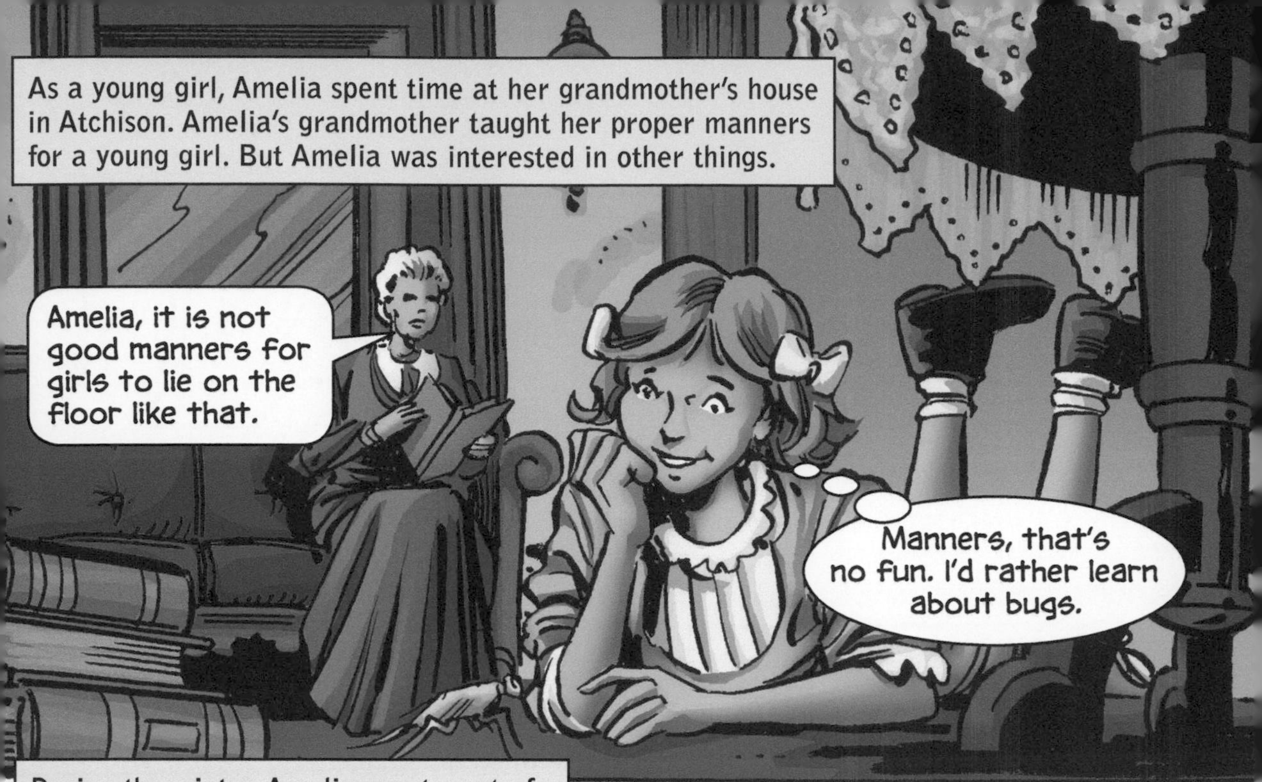
As a young girl, Amelia spent time at her grandmother's house in Atchison. Amelia's grandmother taught her proper manners for a young girl. But Amelia was interested in other things.
Amelia, it is not good manners for girls to lie on the floor like that.
Manners, that's no fun. I'd rather learn about bugs.

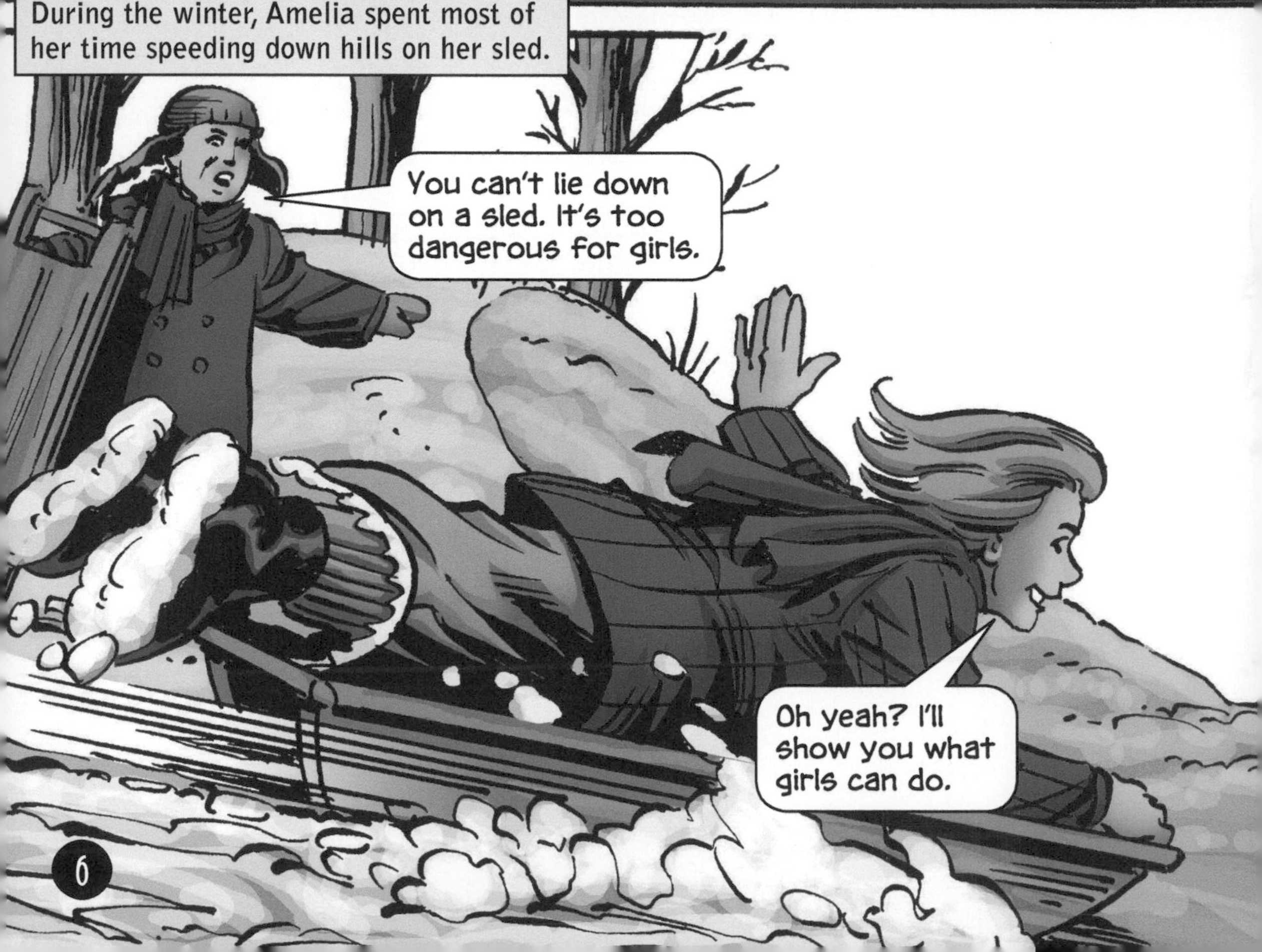
During the winter, Amelia spent most of her time speeding down hills on her sled.
You can't lie down on a sled. It's too dangerous for girls.
Oh yeah? I'll show you what girls can do.

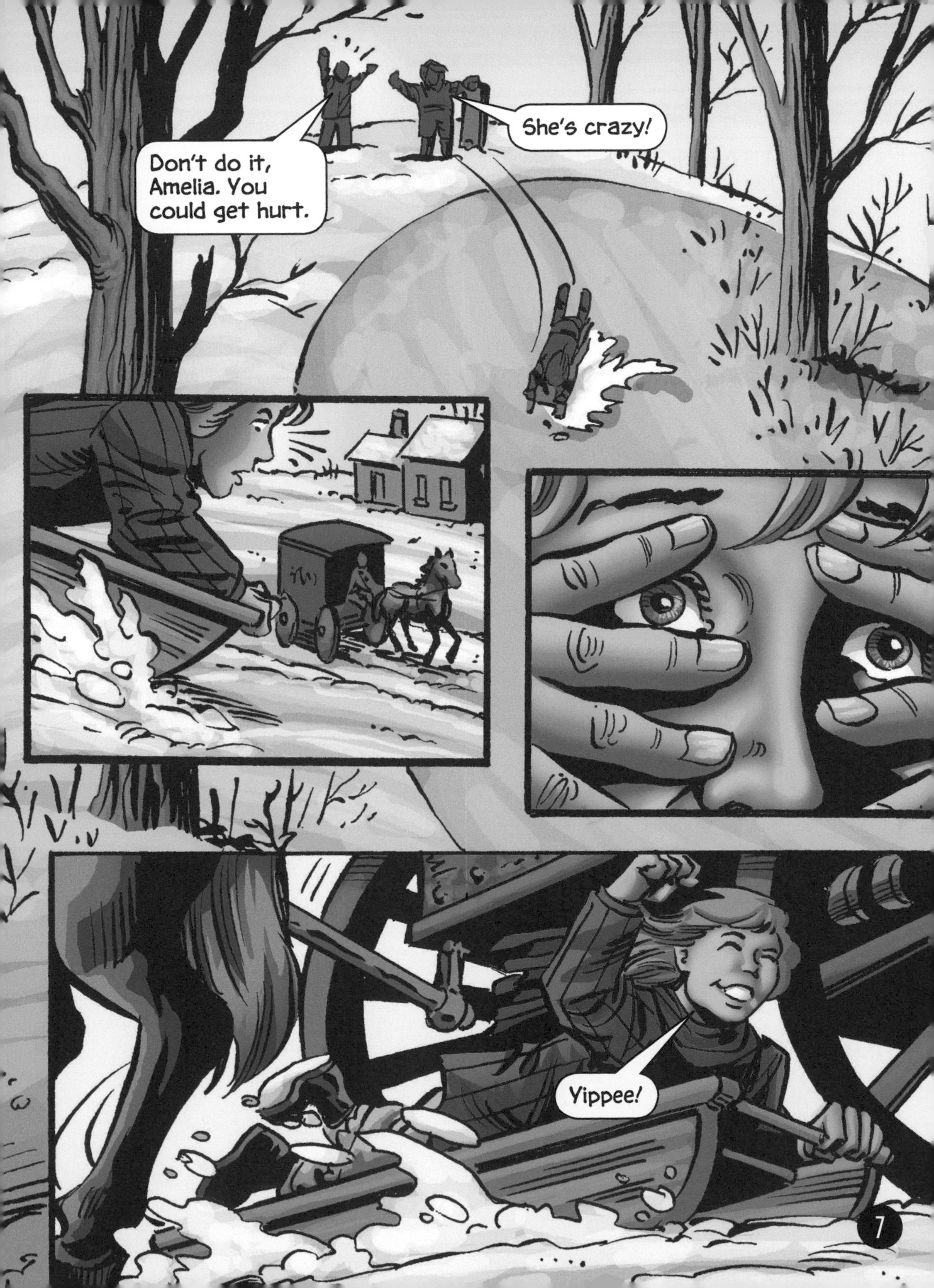
Don't do it, Amelia. You could get hurt.
She's crazy!
Yippee!

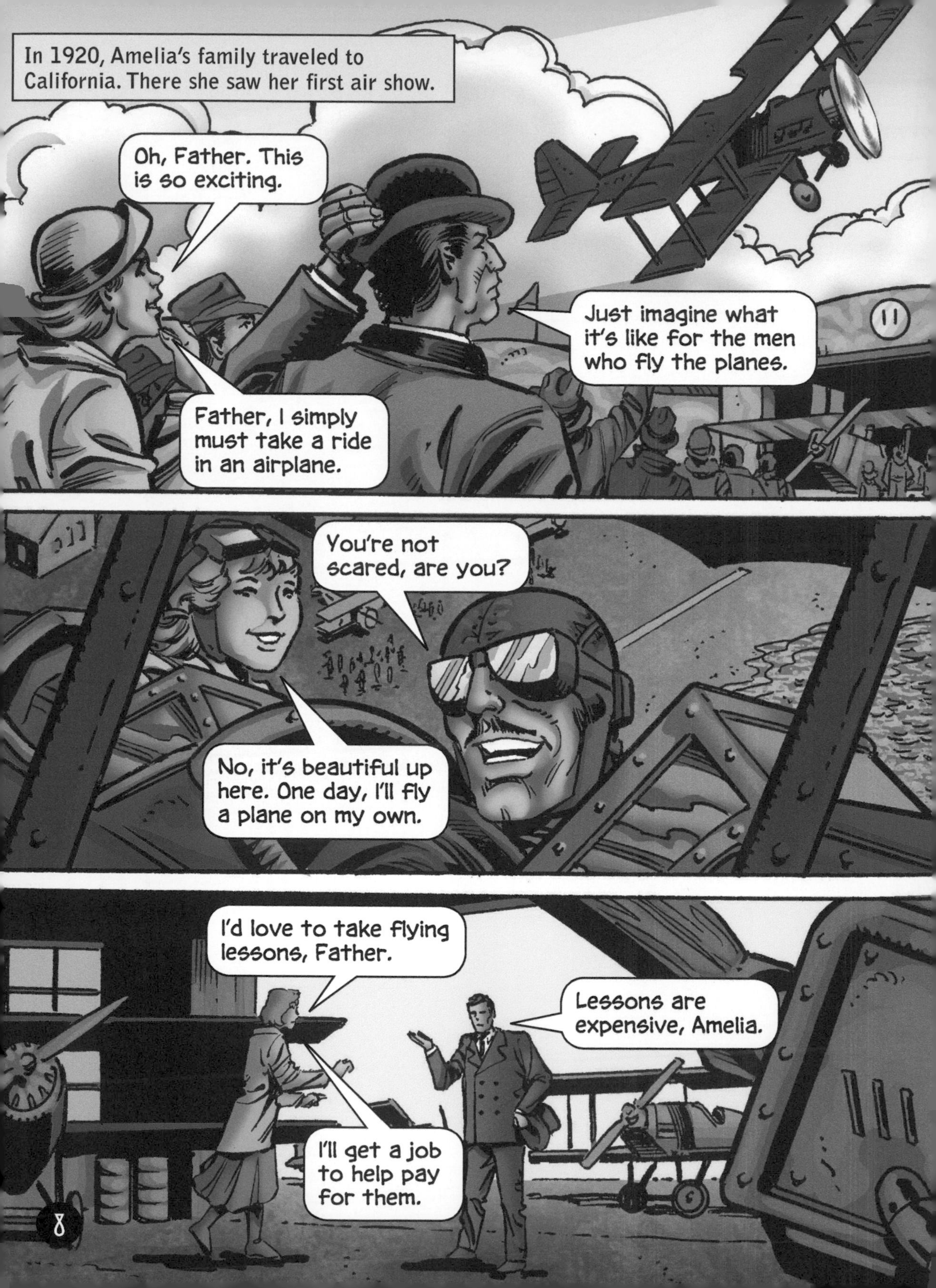
In 1920, Amelia's family traveled to California. There she saw her first air show.
Oh, Father. This is so exciting.
Just imagine what it's like for the men who fly the planes.
Father, I simply must take a ride in an airplane.
You're not scared, are you?
No, it's beautiful up here. One day, I'll fly a plane on my own.
I'd love to take flying lessons, Father.
Lessons are expensive, Amelia.
I'll get a job to help pay for them.

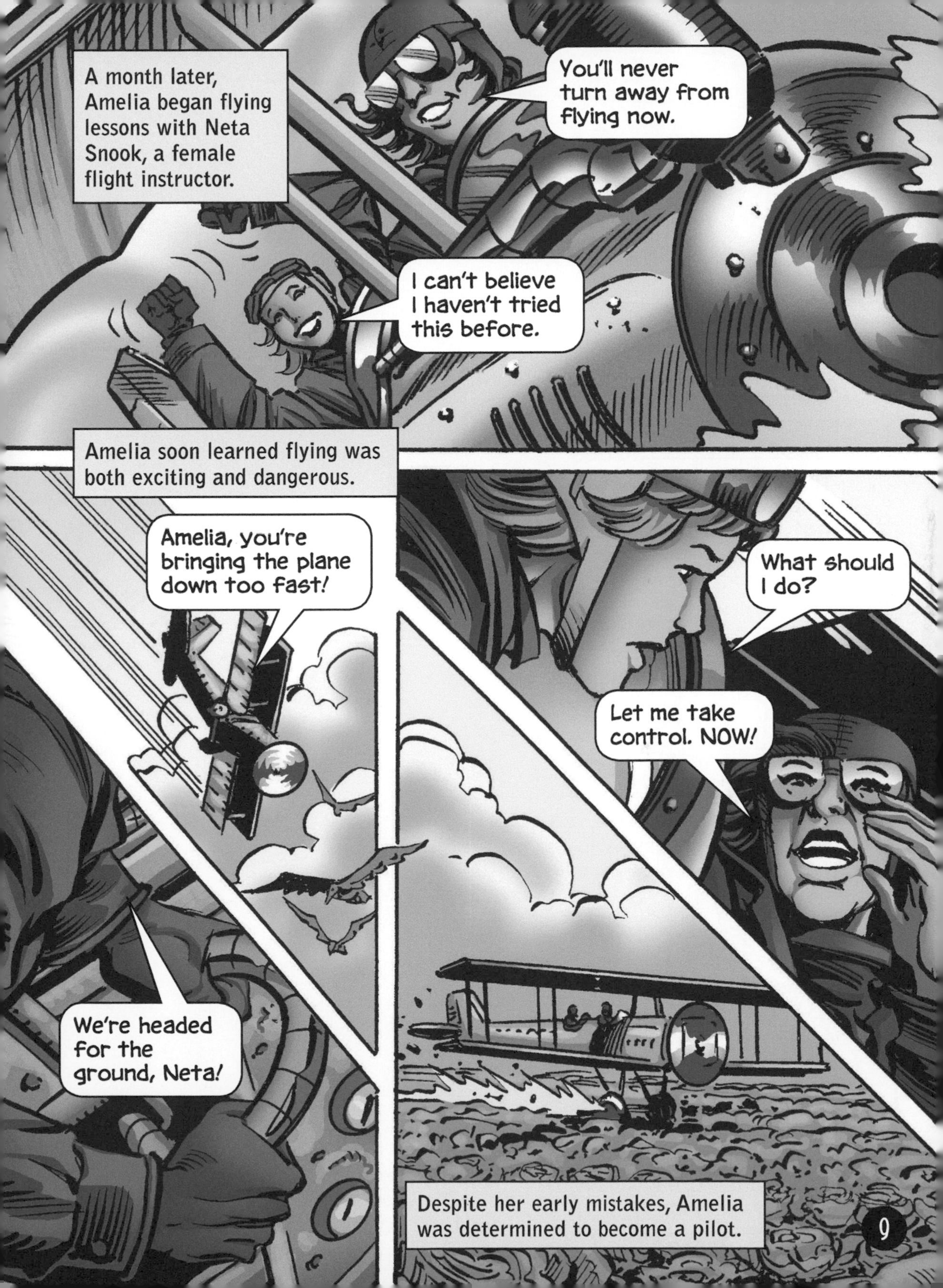
A month later, Amelia began flying lessons with Neta Snook, a female flight instructor.
You'll never turn away from flying now.
I can't believe I haven't tried this before.
Amelia soon learned flying was both exciting and dangerous.
Amelia, you're bringing the plane down too fast!
What should I do?
We're headed for the ground, Neta!
Let me take control. NOW!
Despite her early mistakes, Amelia was determined to become a pilot.

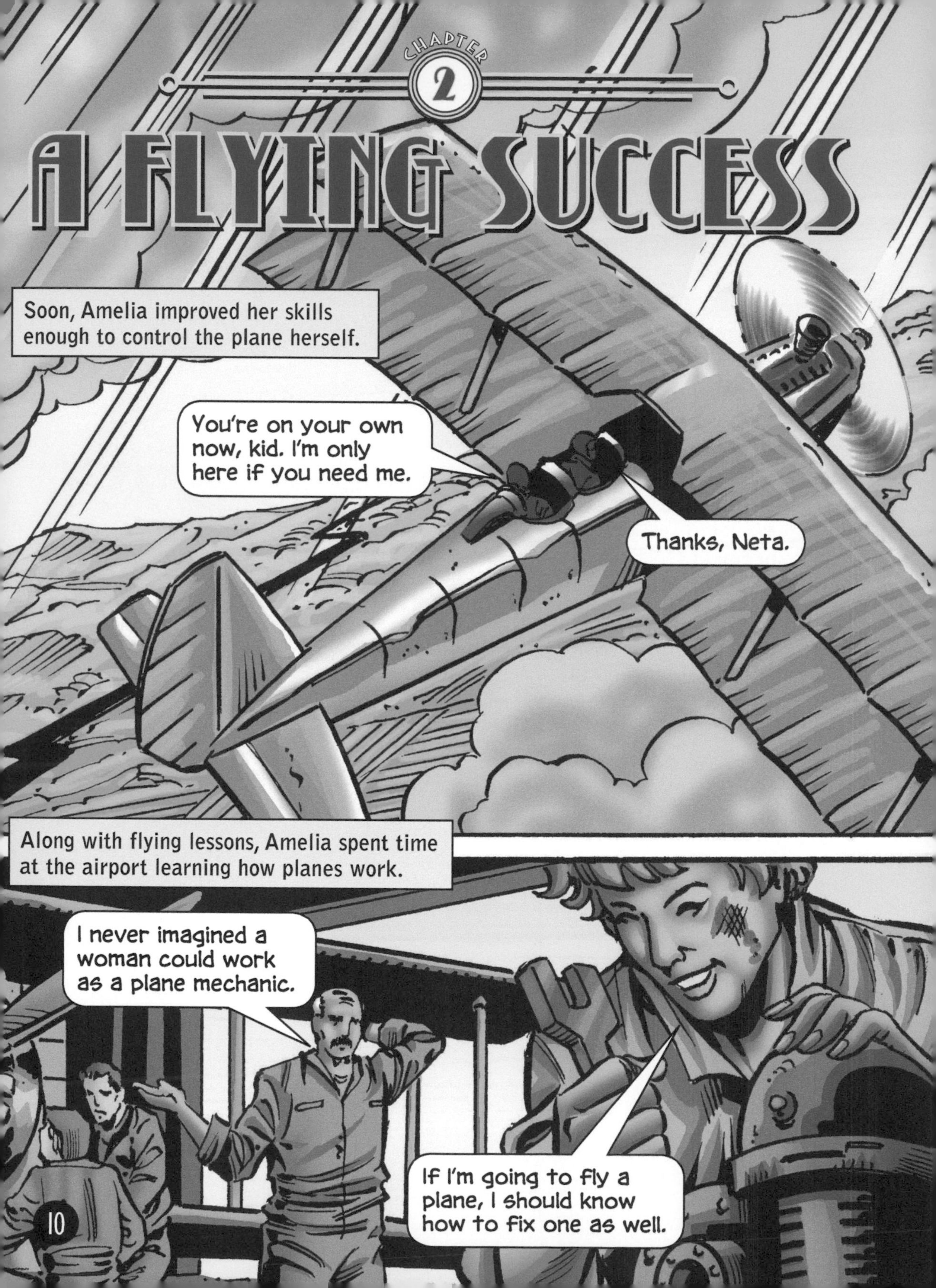
CHAPTER 2
A FLYING SUCCESS
Soon, Amelia improved her skills enough to control the plane herself.
You're on your own now, kid. I'm only here if you need me.
Thanks, Neta.
Along with flying lessons, Amelia spent time at the airport learning how planes work.
I never imagined a woman could work as a plane mechanic.
If I'm going to fly a plane, I should know how to fix one as well.

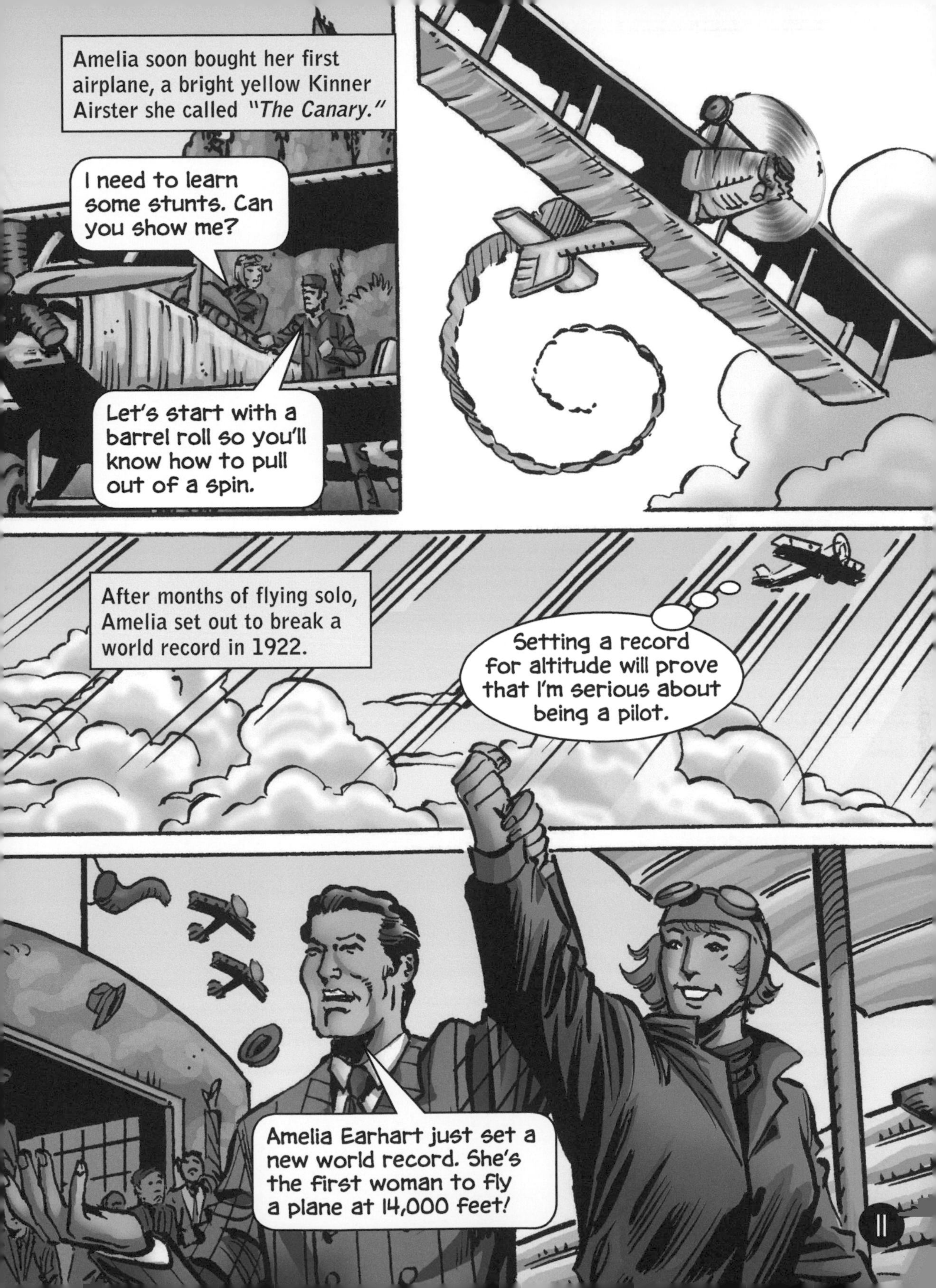
Amelia soon bought her first airplane, a bright yellow Kinner Airster she called *"The Canary."*
I need to learn some stunts. Can you show me?
Let's start with a barrel roll so you'll know how to pull out of a spin.
After months of flying solo, Amelia set out to break a world record in 1922.
Setting a record for altitude will prove that I'm serious about being a pilot.
Amelia Earhart just set a new world record. She's the first woman to fly a plane at 14,000 feet!

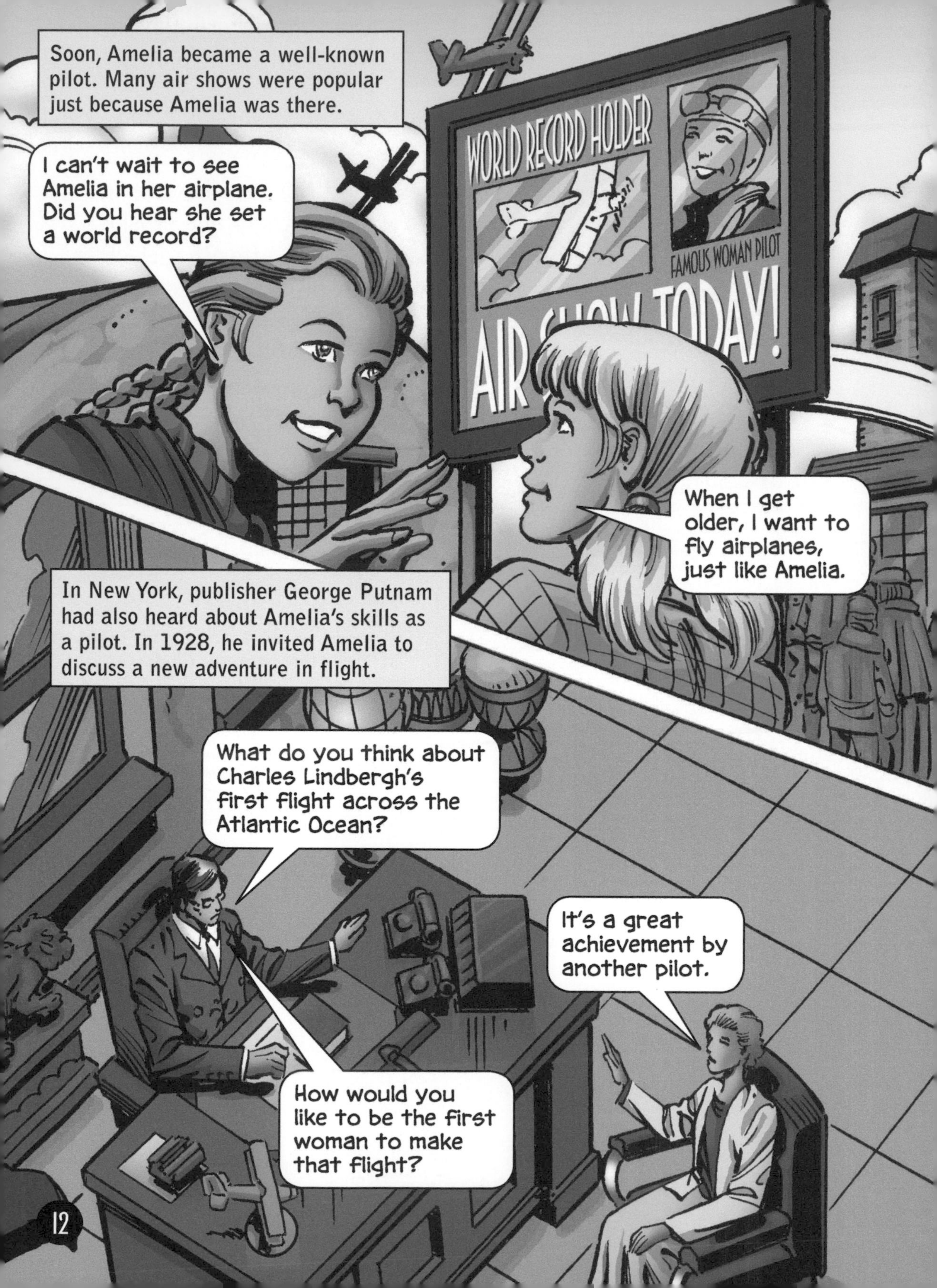

Soon, Amelia became a well-known pilot. Many air shows were popular just because Amelia was there.
I can't wait to see Amelia in her airplane. Did you hear she set a world record?
WORLD RECORD HOLDER
FAMOUS WOMAN PILOT
AIR SHOW TODAY!
When I get older, I want to fly airplanes, just like Amelia.
In New York, publisher George Putnam had also heard about Amelia's skills as a pilot. In 1928, he invited Amelia to discuss a new adventure in flight.
What do you think about Charles Lindbergh's first flight across the Atlantic Ocean?
It's a great achievement by another pilot.
How would you like to be the first woman to make that flight?

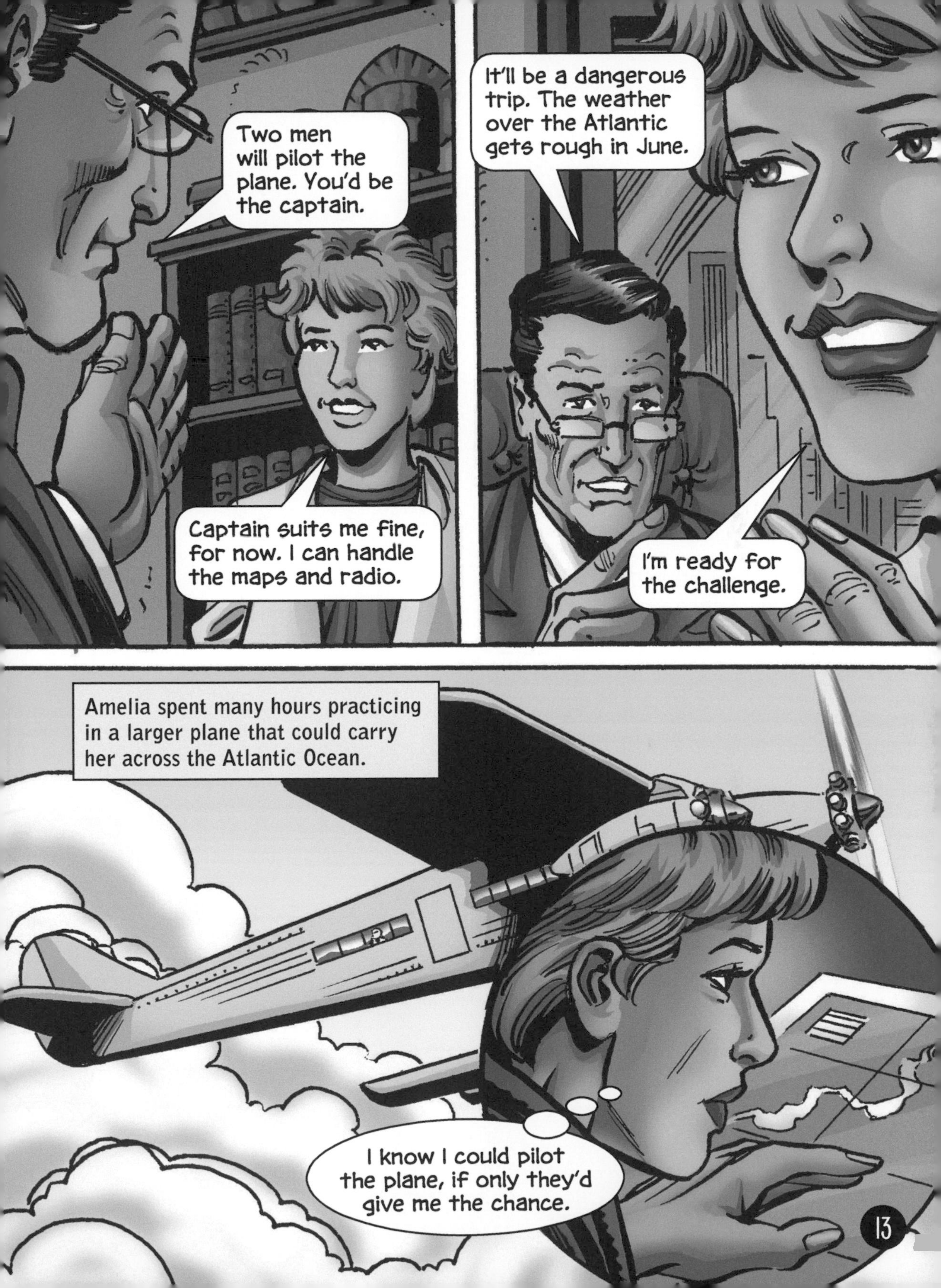
Two men will pilot the plane. You'd be the captain.
Captain suits me fine, for now. I can handle the maps and radio.
It'll be a dangerous trip. The weather over the Atlantic gets rough in June.
I'm ready for the challenge.
Amelia spent many hours practicing in a larger plane that could carry her across the Atlantic Ocean.
I know I could pilot the plane, if only they'd give me the chance.

Chapter 3
A Strong Woman

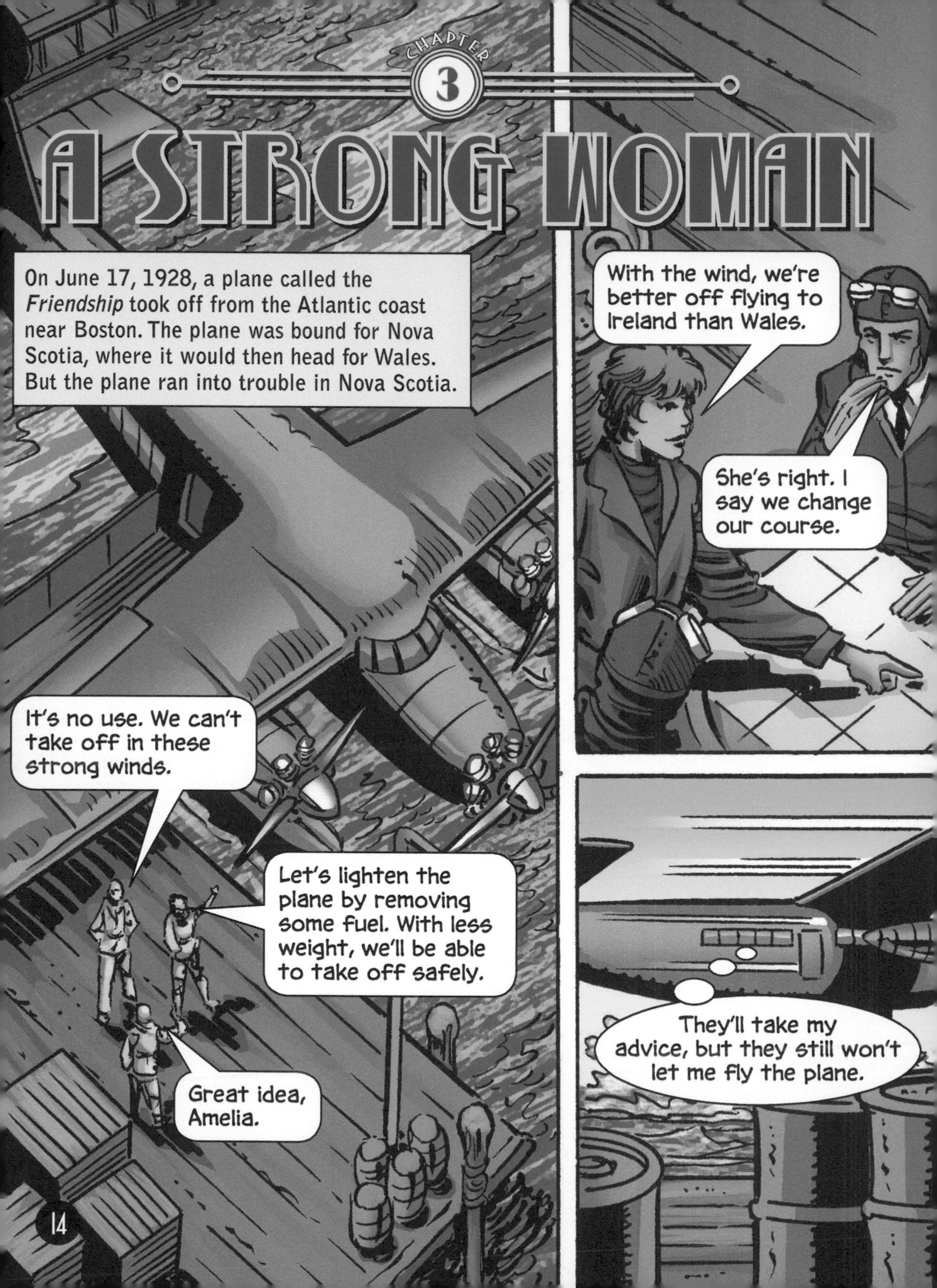
On June 17, 1928, a plane called the *Friendship* took off from the Atlantic coast near Boston. The plane was bound for Nova Scotia, where it would then head for Wales. But the plane ran into trouble in Nova Scotia.
It's no use. We can't take off in these strong winds.
Let's lighten the plane by removing some fuel. With less weight, we'll be able to take off safely.
Great idea, Amelia.
With the wind, we're better off flying to Ireland than Wales.
She's right. I say we change our course.
They'll take my advice, but they still won't let me fly the plane.

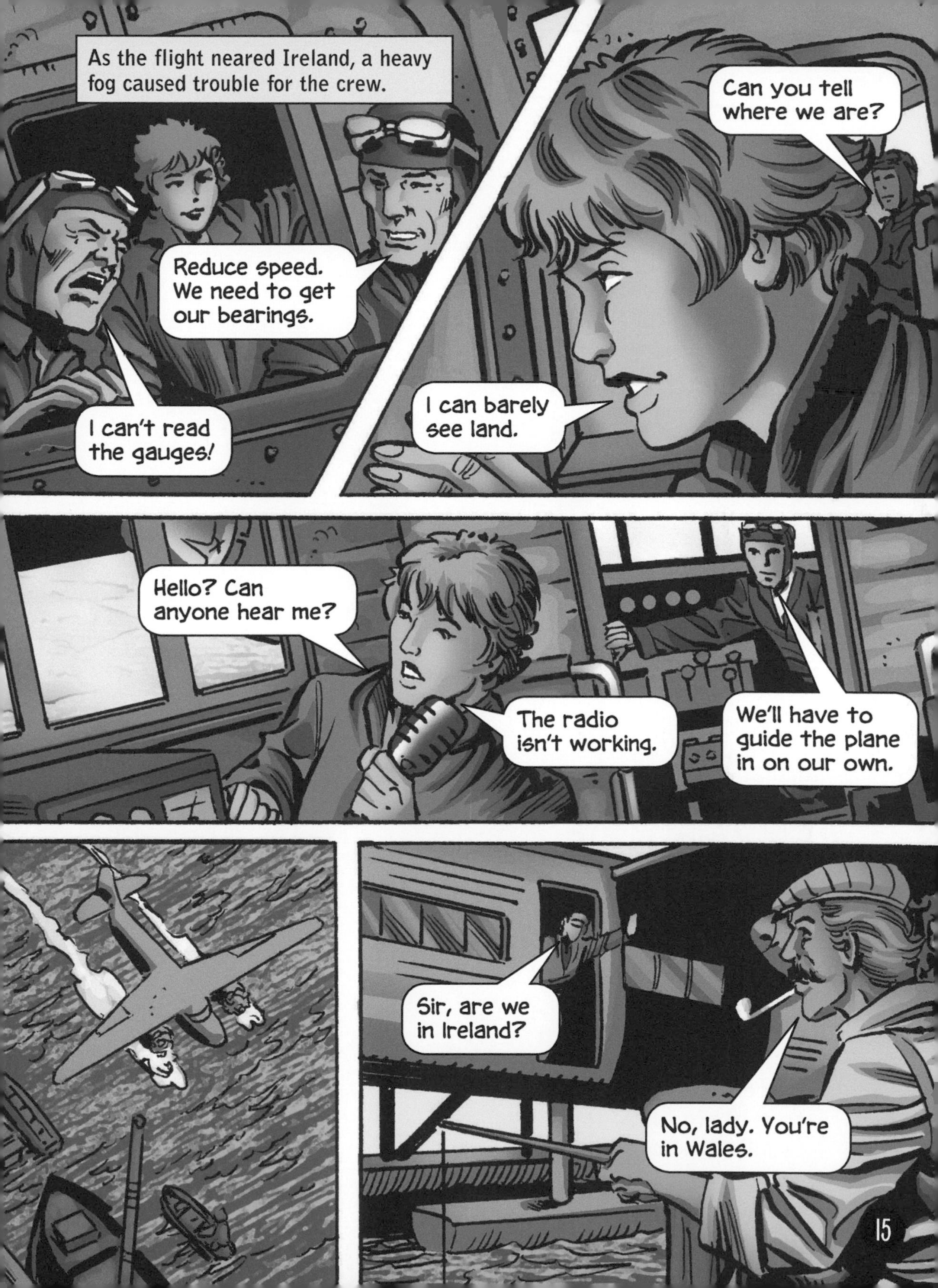
As the flight neared Ireland, a heavy fog caused trouble for the crew.
Reduce speed. We need to get our bearings.
I can't read the gauges!
Can you tell where we are?
I can barely see land.
Hello? Can anyone hear me?
The radio isn't working.
We'll have to guide the plane in on our own.
Sir, are we in Ireland?
No, lady. You're in Wales.

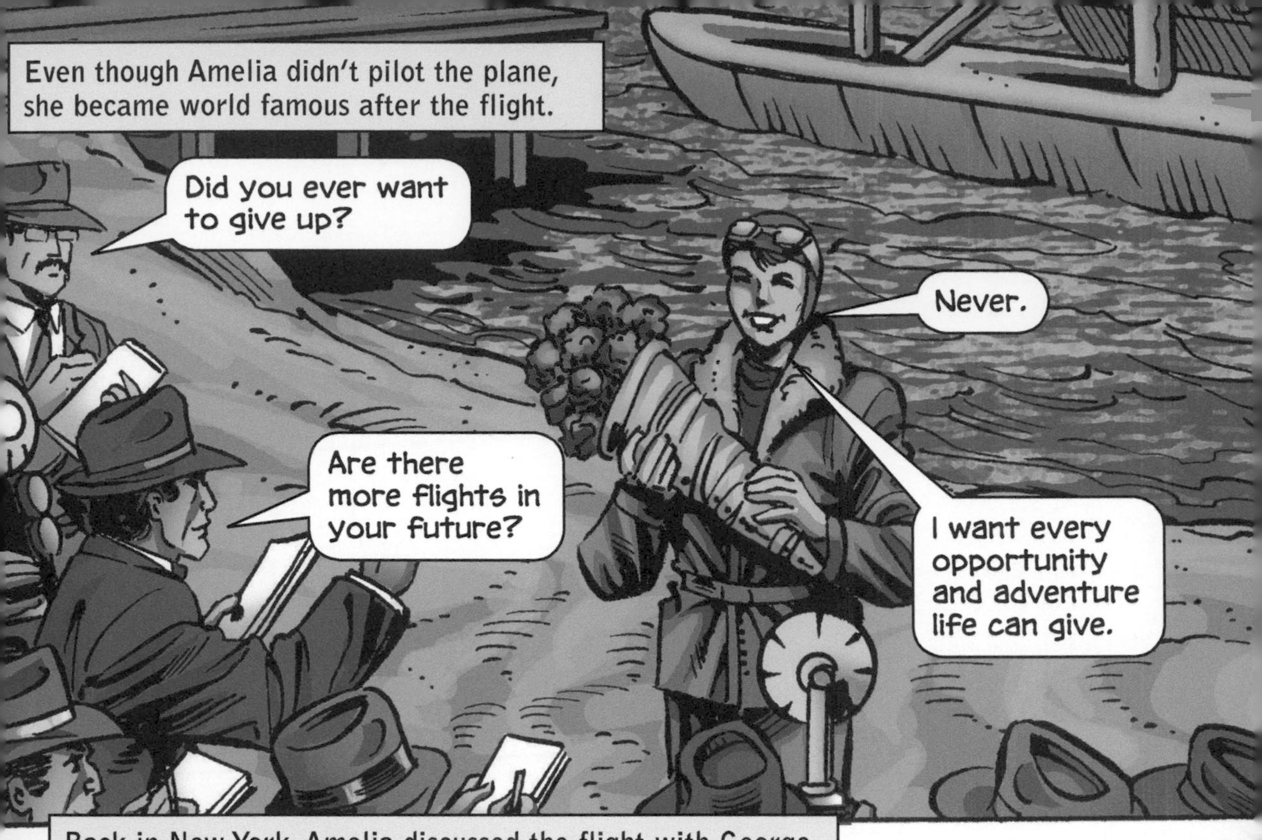
Even though Amelia didn't pilot the plane, she became world famous after the flight.
Did you ever want to give up?
Never.
Are there more flights in your future?
I want every opportunity and adventure life can give.

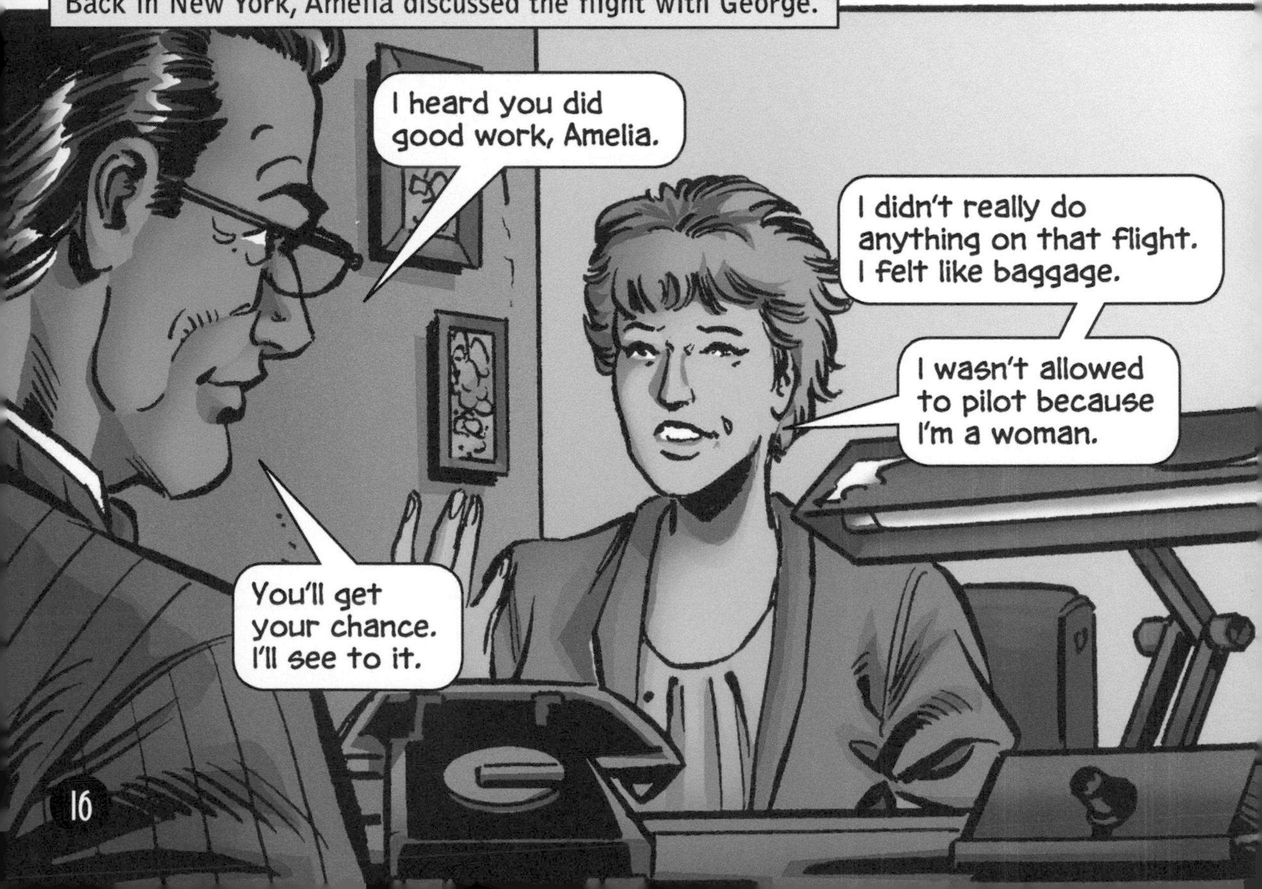
Back in New York, Amelia discussed the flight with George.
I heard you did good work, Amelia.
I didn't really do anything on that flight. I felt like baggage.
I wasn't allowed to pilot because I'm a woman.
You'll get your chance. I'll see to it.

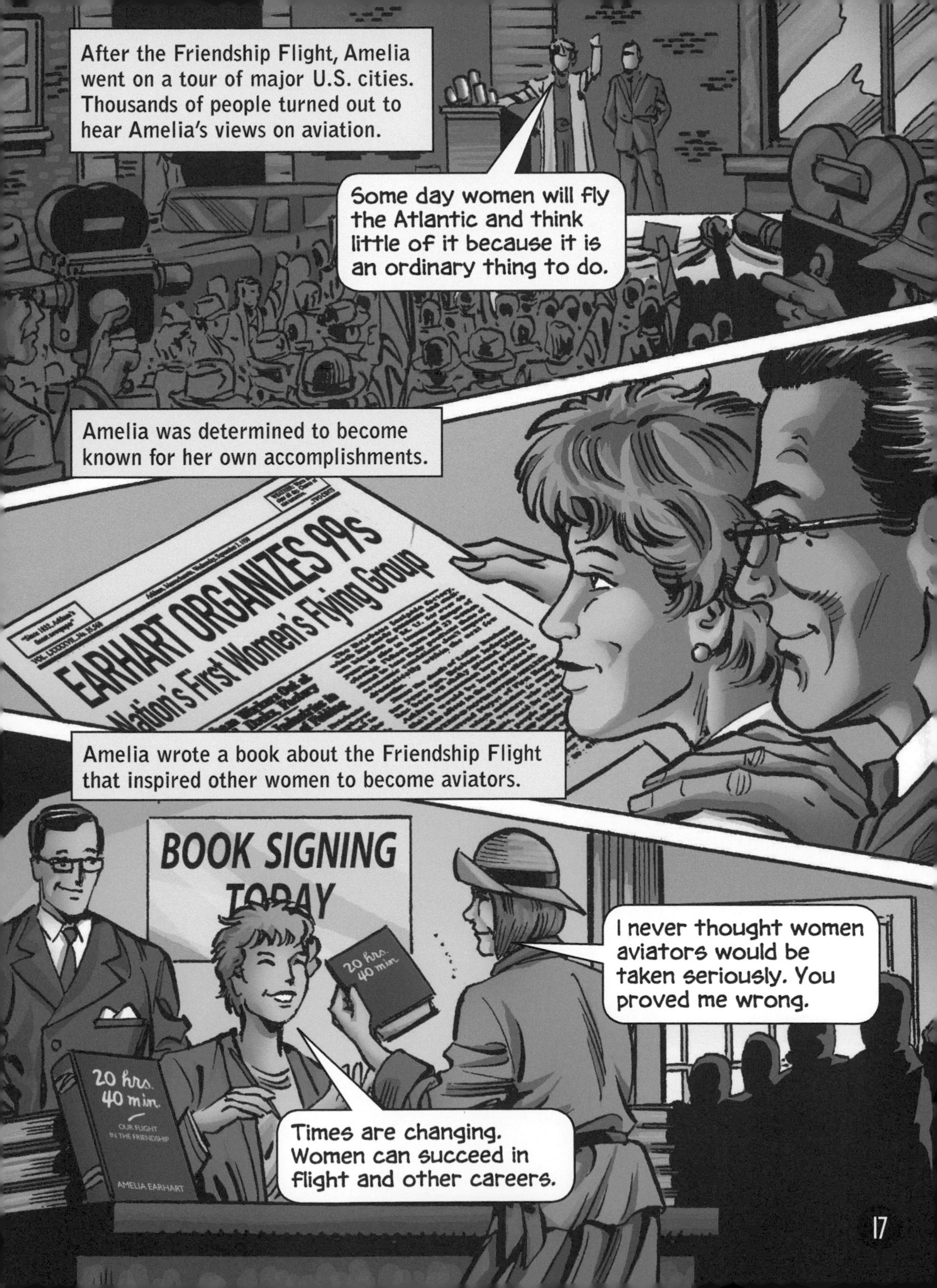
After the Friendship Flight, Amelia went on a tour of major U.S. cities. Thousands of people turned out to hear Amelia's views on aviation.
Some day women will fly the Atlantic and think little of it because it is an ordinary thing to do.
Amelia was determined to become known for her own accomplishments.
EARHART ORGANIZES 99s
Nation's First Women's Flying Group
Amelia wrote a book about the Friendship Flight that inspired other women to become aviators.
BOOK SIGNING TODAY
20 hrs. 40 min.
20 hrs. 40 min. OUR FLIGHT IN THE FRIENDSHIP AMELIA EARHART
I never thought women aviators would be taken seriously. You proved me wrong.
Times are changing. Women can succeed in flight and other careers.

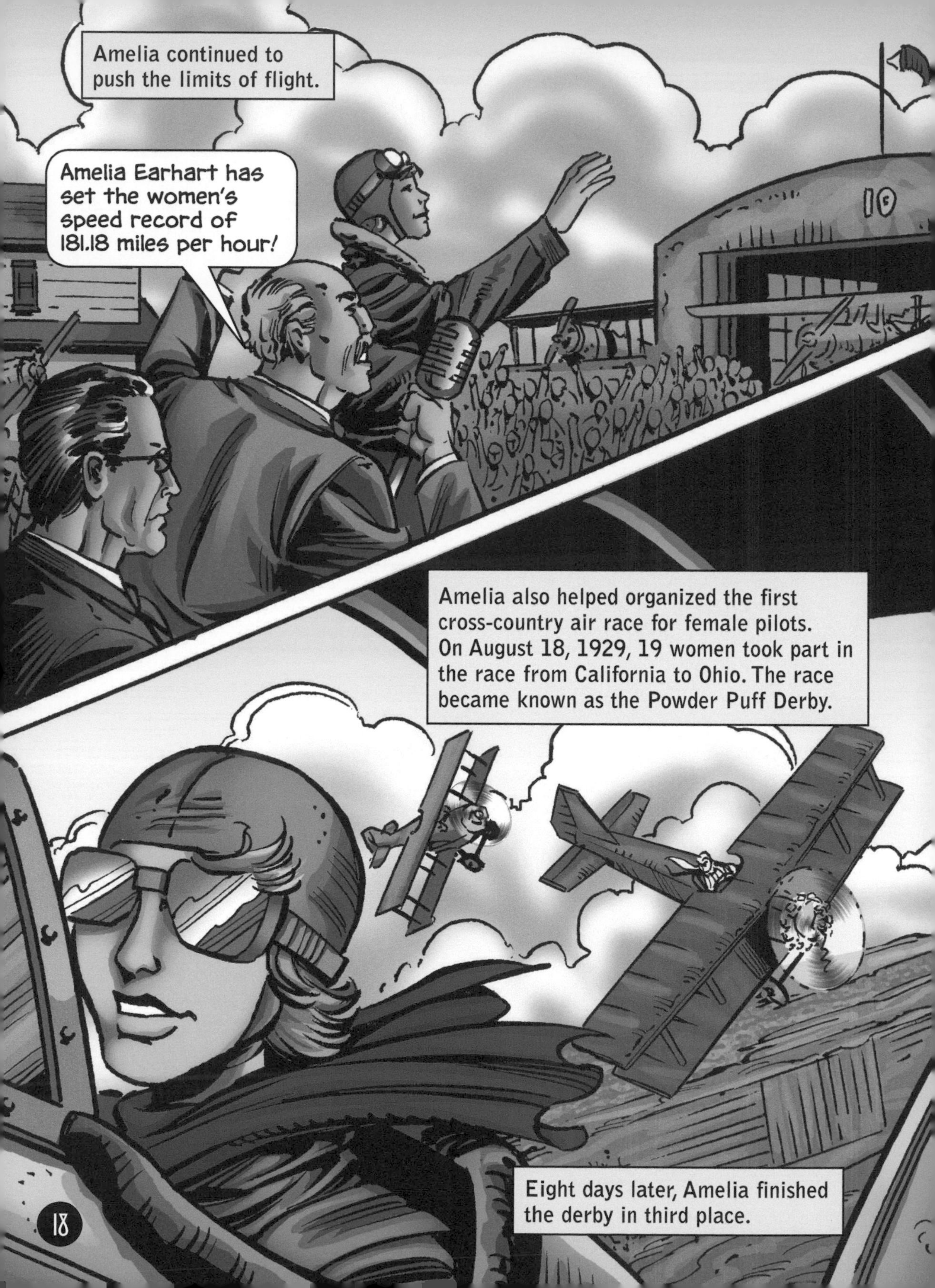
Amelia continued to push the limits of flight.
Amelia Earhart has set the women's speed record of 181.18 miles per hour!
Amelia also helped organized the first cross-country air race for female pilots. On August 18, 1929, 19 women took part in the race from California to Ohio. The race became known as the Powder Puff Derby.
Eight days later, Amelia finished the derby in third place.

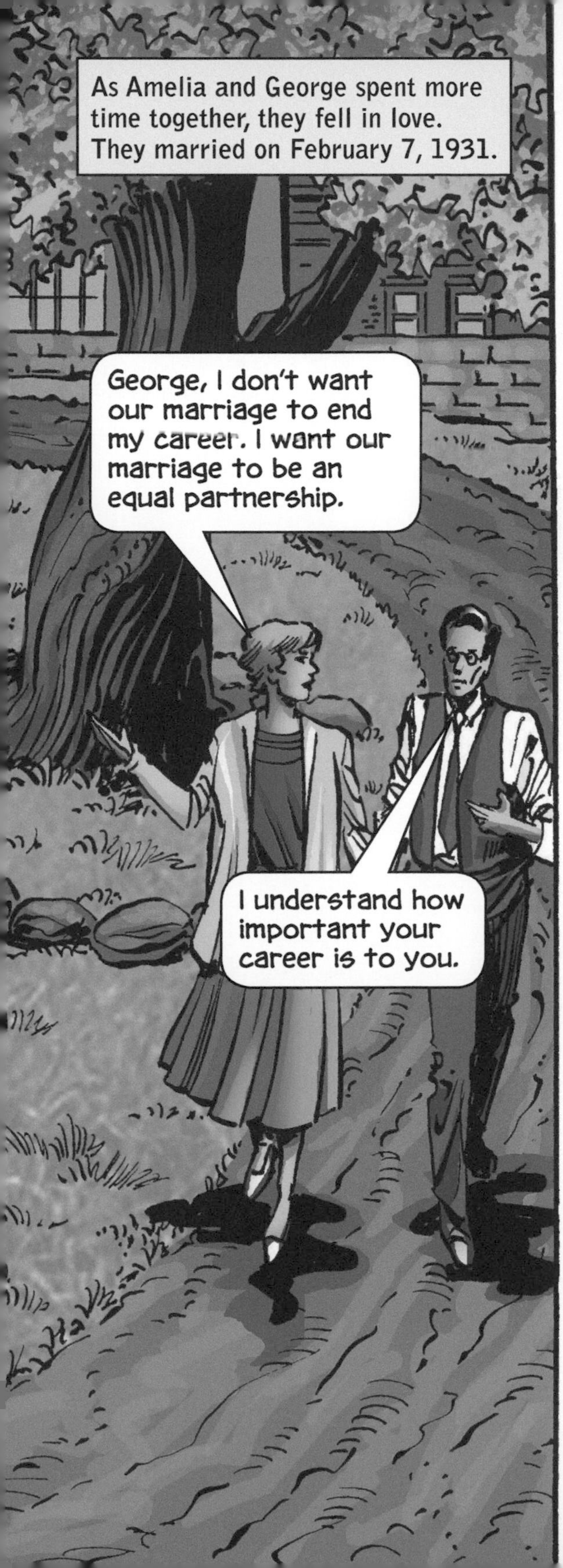
As Amelia and George spent more time together, they fell in love. They married on February 7, 1931.
George, I don't want our marriage to end my career. I want our marriage to be an equal partnership.
I understand how important your career is to you.

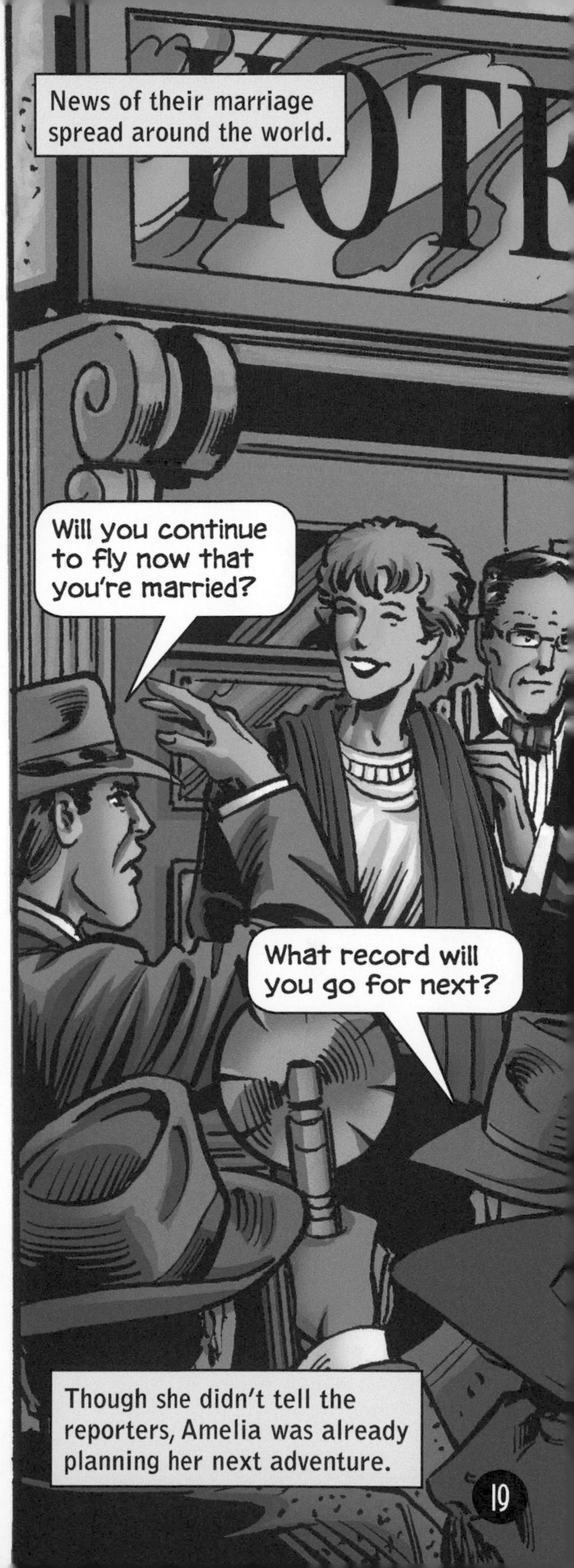
News of their marriage spread around the world.
Will you continue to fly now that you're married?
What record will you go for next?
Though she didn't tell the reporters, Amelia was already planning her next adventure.

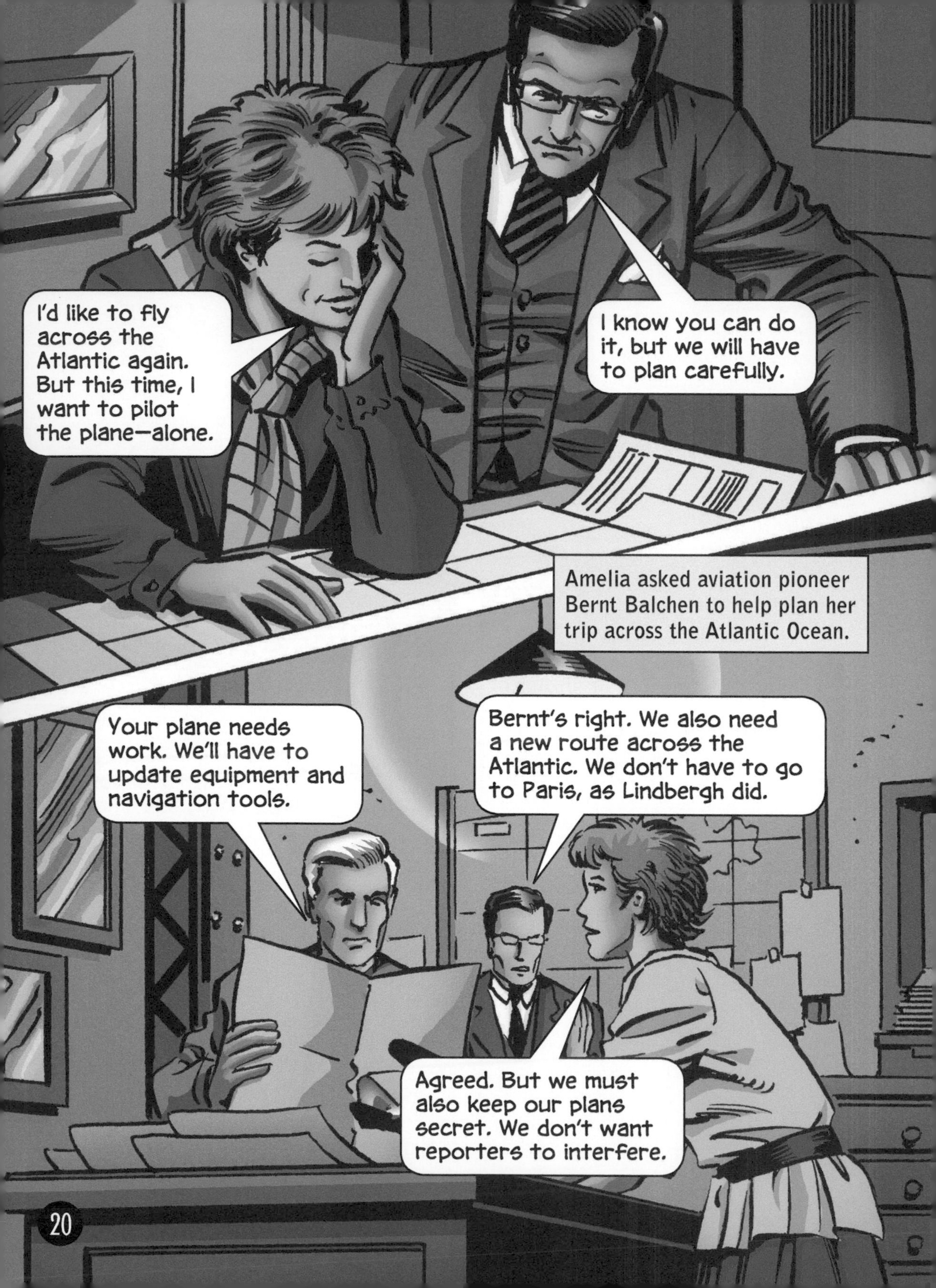
I'd like to fly across the Atlantic again. But this time, I want to pilot the plane—alone.
I know you can do it, but we will have to plan carefully.
Amelia asked aviation pioneer Bernt Balchen to help plan her trip across the Atlantic Ocean.
Your plane needs work. We'll have to update equipment and navigation tools.
Bernt's right. We also need a new route across the Atlantic. We don't have to go to Paris, as Lindbergh did.
Agreed. But we must also keep our plans secret. We don't want reporters to interfere.

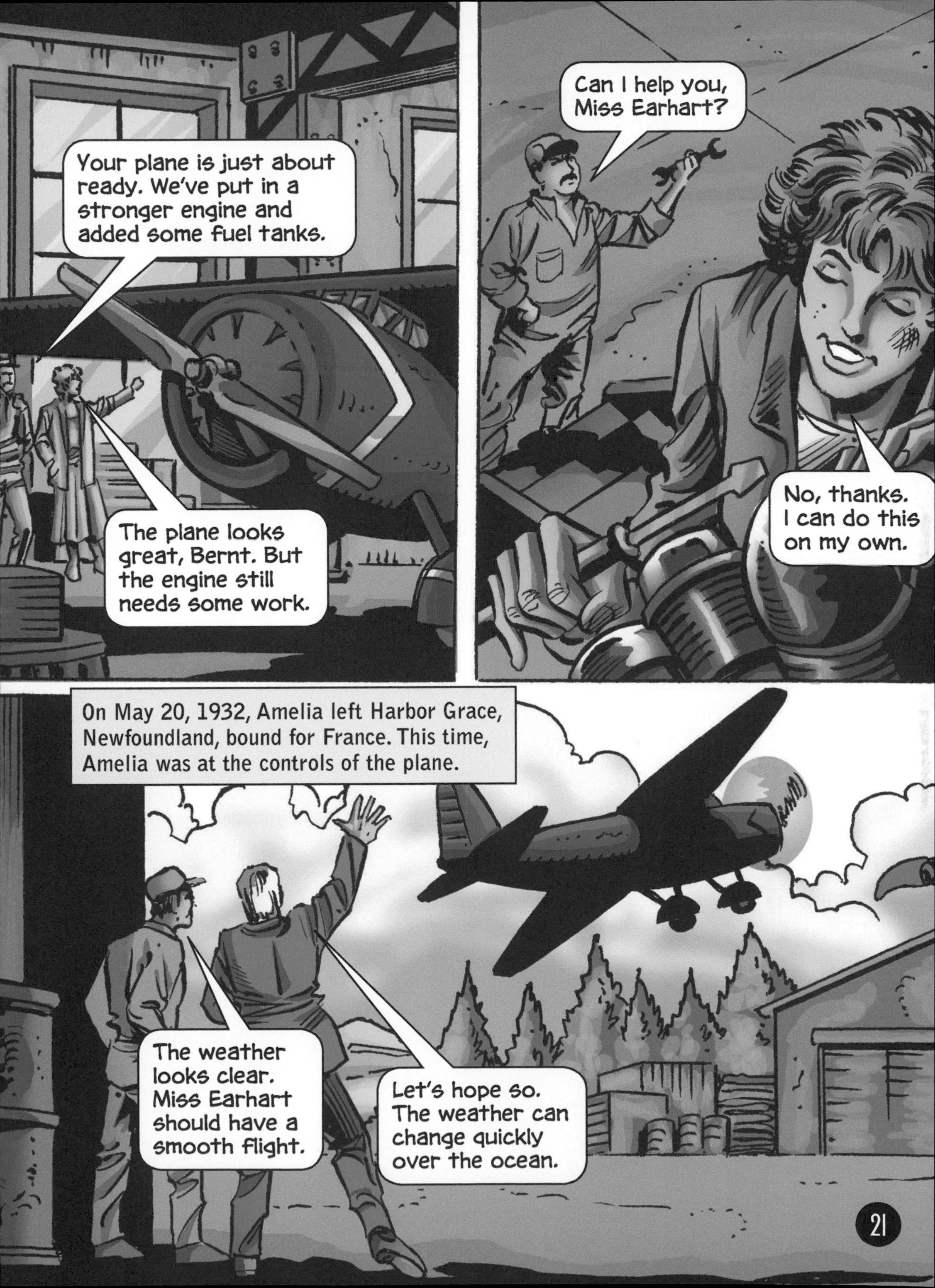

Your plane is just about ready. We've put in a stronger engine and added some fuel tanks.
The plane looks great, Bernt. But the engine still needs some work.
Can I help you, Miss Earhart?
No, thanks. I can do this on my own.
On May 20, 1932, Amelia left Harbor Grace, Newfoundland, bound for France. This time, Amelia was at the controls of the plane.
The weather looks clear. Miss Earhart should have a smooth flight.
Let's hope so. The weather can change quickly over the ocean.

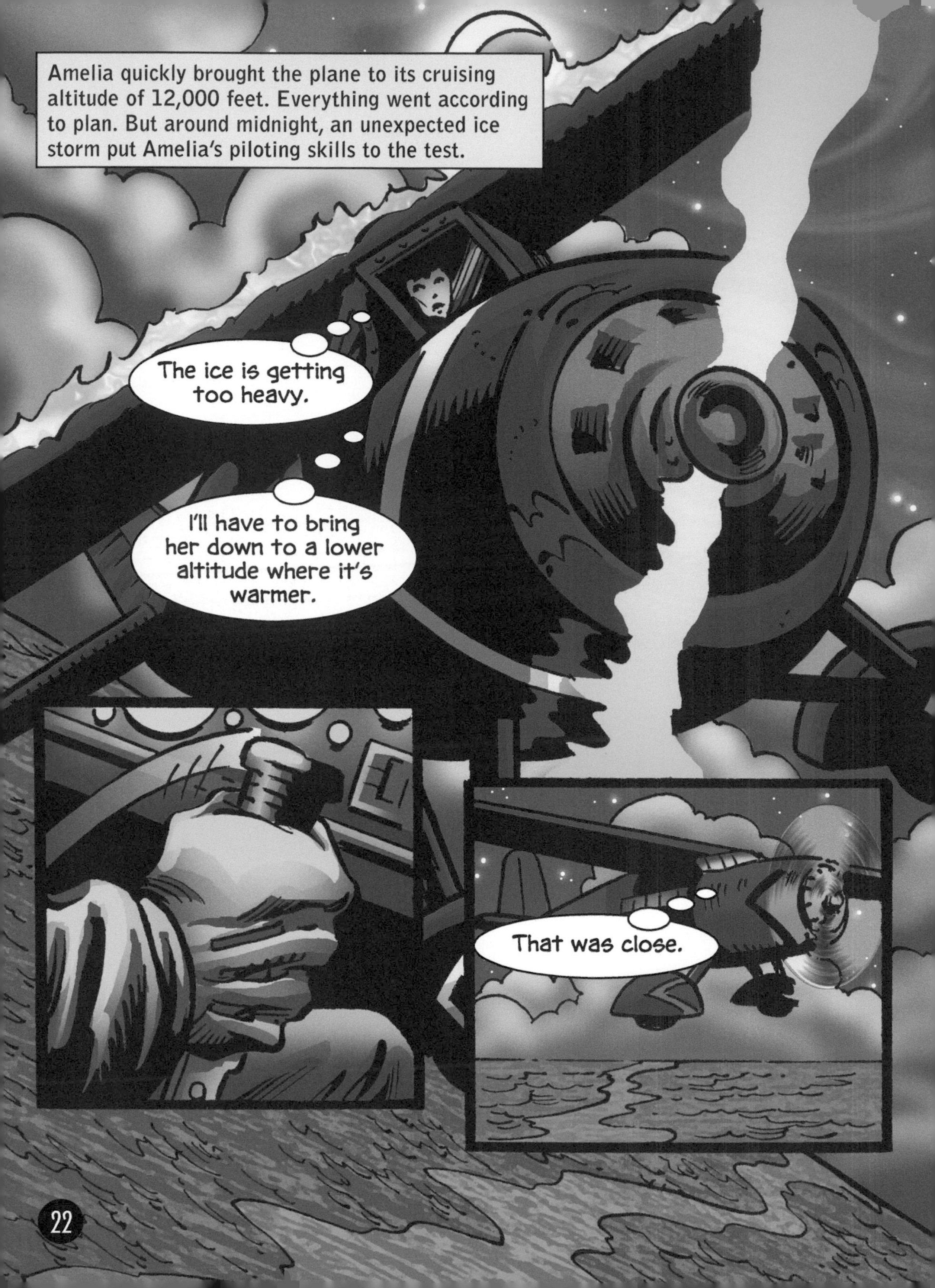
Amelia quickly brought the plane to its cruising altitude of 12,000 feet. Everything went according to plan. But around midnight, an unexpected ice storm put Amelia's piloting skills to the test.
The ice is getting too heavy.
I'll have to bring her down to a lower altitude where it's warmer.
That was close.

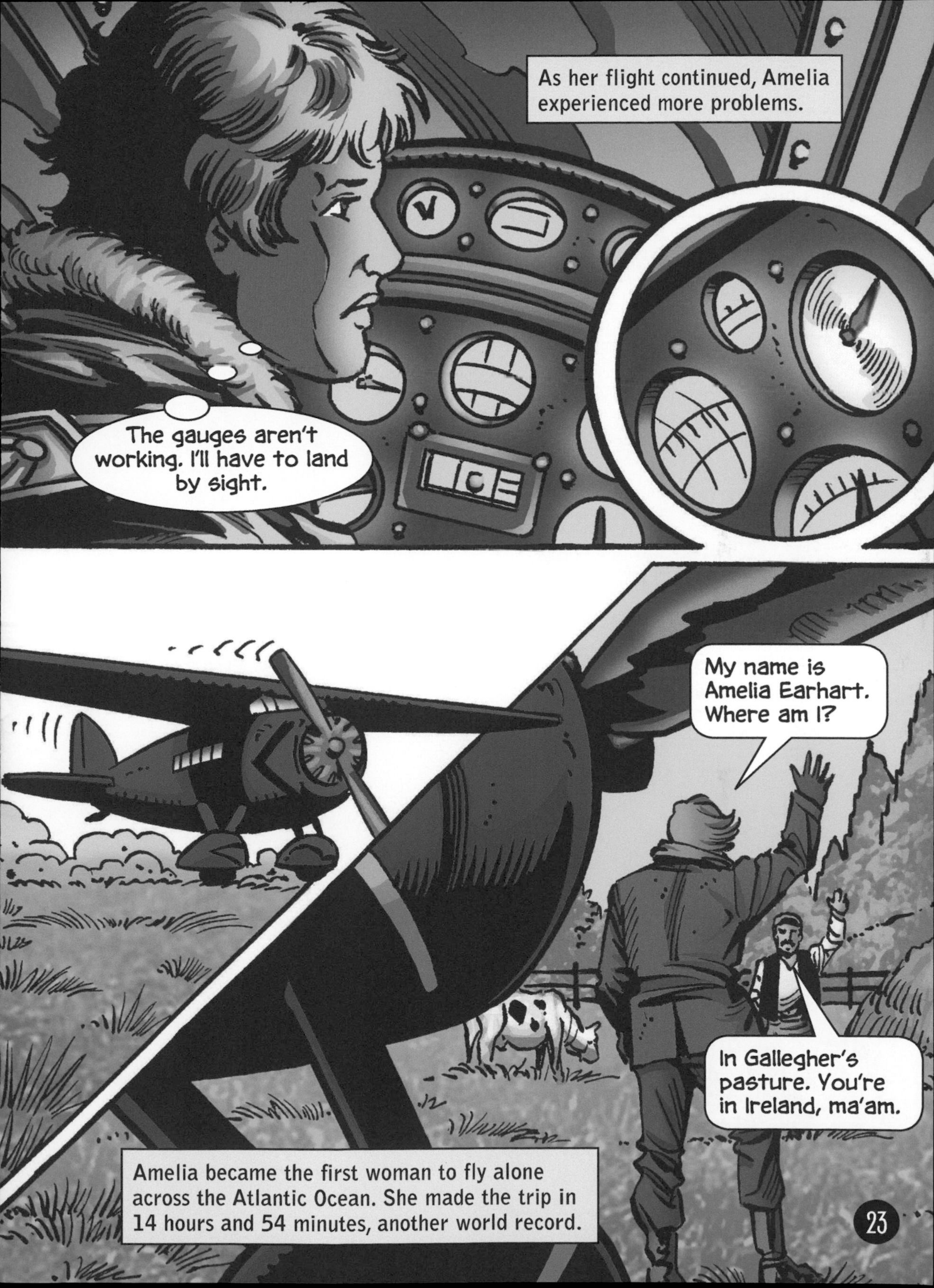
As her flight continued, Amelia experienced more problems.
The gauges aren't working. I'll have to land by sight.
My name is Amelia Earhart. Where am I?
In Gallegher's pasture. You're in Ireland, ma'am.
Amelia became the first woman to fly alone across the Atlantic Ocean. She made the trip in 14 hours and 54 minutes, another world record.

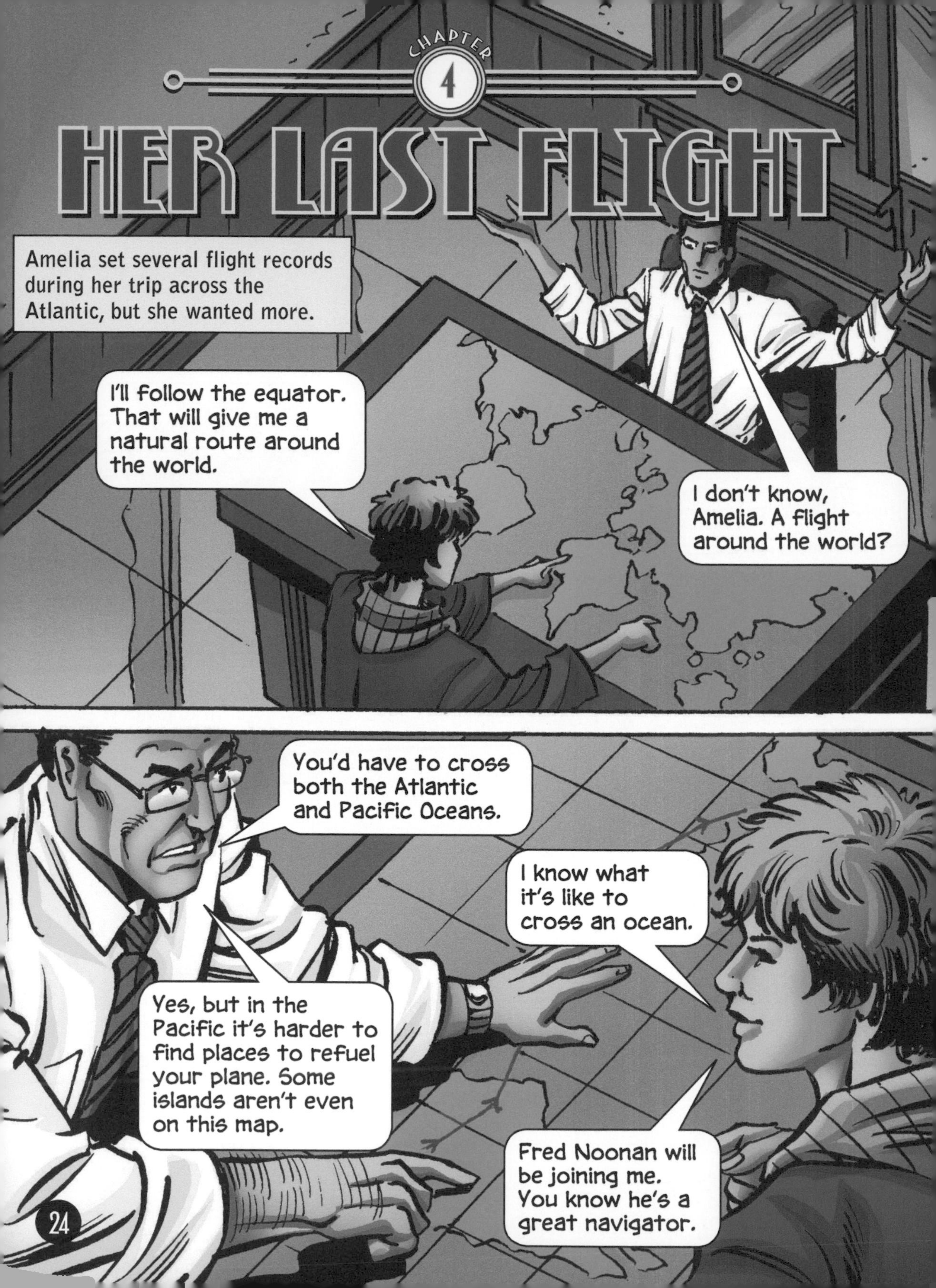
CHAPTER 4
HER LAST FLIGHT
Amelia set several flight records during her trip across the Atlantic, but she wanted more.
I'll follow the equator. That will give me a natural route around the world.
I don't know, Amelia. A flight around the world?
You'd have to cross both the Atlantic and Pacific Oceans.
I know what it's like to cross an ocean.
Yes, but in the Pacific it's harder to find places to refuel your plane. Some islands aren't even on this map.
Fred Noonan will be joining me. You know he's a great navigator.

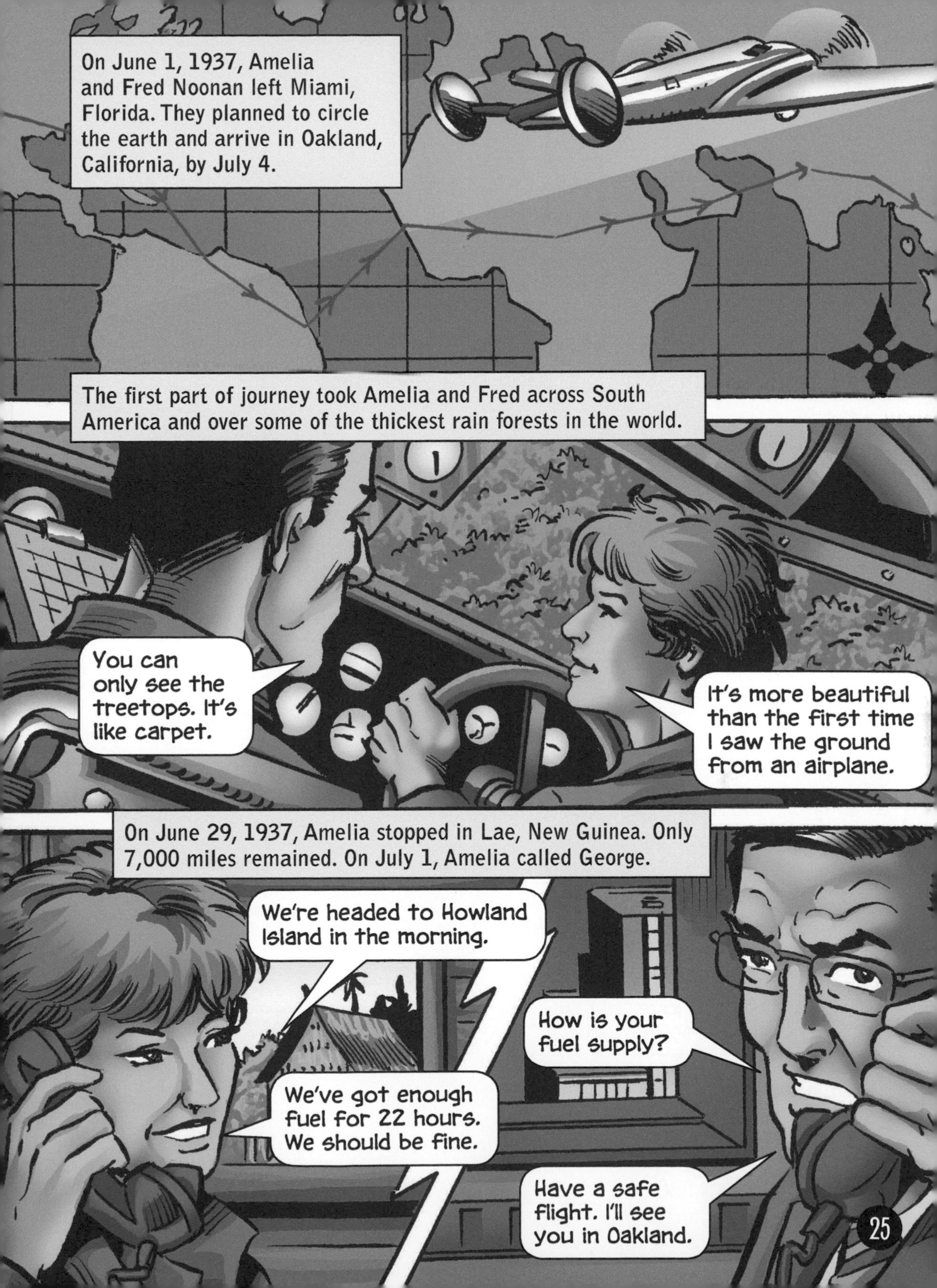
On June 1, 1937, Amelia and Fred Noonan left Miami, Florida. They planned to circle the earth and arrive in Oakland, California, by July 4.
The first part of journey took Amelia and Fred across South America and over some of the thickest rain forests in the world.
You can only see the treetops. It's like carpet.
It's more beautiful than the first time I saw the ground from an airplane.
On June 29, 1937, Amelia stopped in Lae, New Guinea. Only 7,000 miles remained. On July 1, Amelia called George.
We're headed to Howland Island in the morning.
How is your fuel supply?
We've got enough fuel for 22 hours. We should be fine.
Have a safe flight. I'll see you in Oakland.

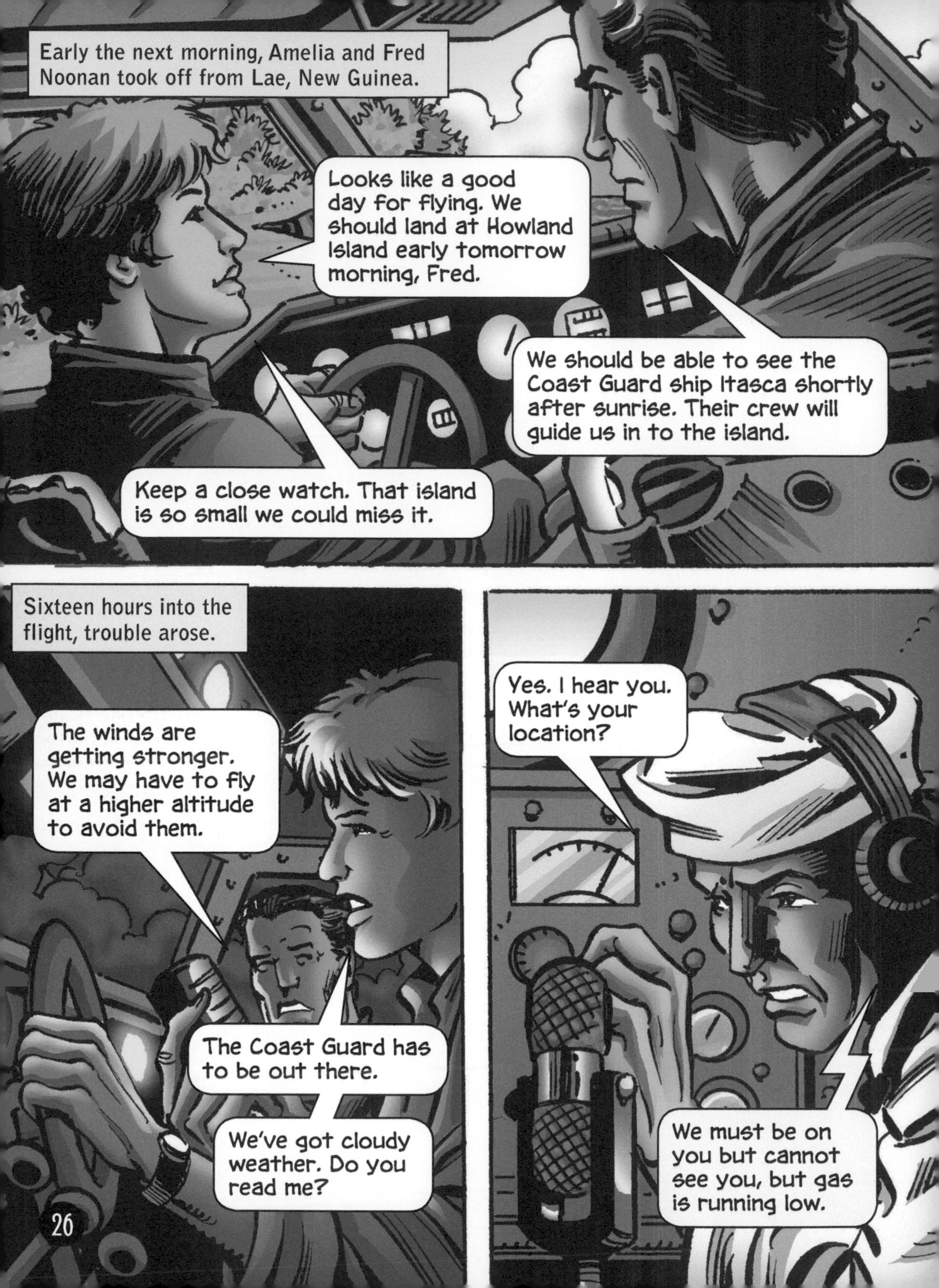
Early the next morning, Amelia and Fred Noonan took off from Lae, New Guinea.
Looks like a good day for flying. We should land at Howland Island early tomorrow morning, Fred.
We should be able to see the Coast Guard ship Itasca shortly after sunrise. Their crew will guide us in to the island.
Keep a close watch. That island is so small we could miss it.
Sixteen hours into the flight, trouble arose.
The winds are getting stronger. We may have to fly at a higher altitude to avoid them.
The Coast Guard has to be out there.
We've got cloudy weather. Do you read me?
Yes. I hear you. What's your location?
We must be on you but cannot see you, but gas is running low.

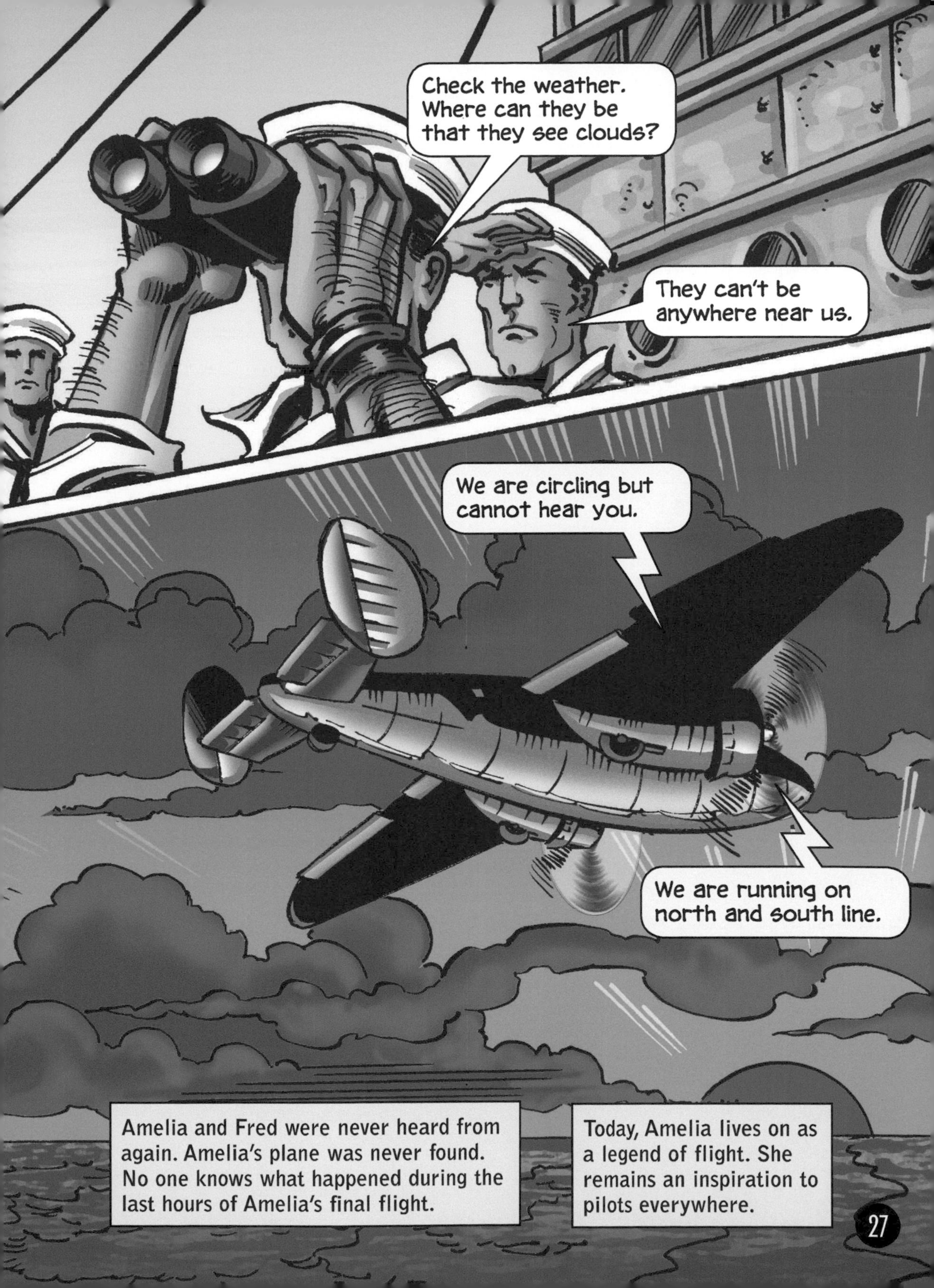
Check the weather. Where can they be that they see clouds?
They can't be anywhere near us.
We are circling but cannot hear you.
We are running on north and south line.
Amelia and Fred were never heard from again. Amelia's plane was never found. No one knows what happened during the last hours of Amelia's final flight.
Today, Amelia lives on as a legend of flight. She remains an inspiration to pilots everywhere.

AMELIA EARHART

- Amelia Earhart was born July 24, 1897, in Atchison, Kansas.

- Amelia saw her first airplane at a fair in Iowa. "It's just rusty wire and wood. It's not at all interesting," she said.

- It took Amelia 14 hours and 54 minutes to cross the Atlantic Ocean during her solo flight. Today, planes can make that same trip in about seven hours.

- Amelia's solo flight across the Atlantic was very dangerous. At one point, a broken piece of an engine ring caught on fire. The fire went out, but not before it damaged the metal of Amelia's plane.

- Amelia wrote three books about her aviation career. Her book *20 hrs. 40 min.* tells the story of the Friendship Flight. In *For the Fun of It*, Amelia writes about her love for adventure and flight. Her final book, *Last Flight*, was published by her husband shortly after Amelia disappeared. This book includes accounts of Amelia's final flight up until she and Fred left Lae, New Guinea.

- In 1931, Amelia became the first president of the Ninety Nines, a women's flying group that is still active today.

- After Amelia's plane went missing, the U.S. government spent $4 million on the search for her, Fred, and their airplane.

- People have come up with many ideas about what happened to Amelia on her final flight. Some believe Amelia's Lockheed Electra ran out of gas and crashed into the Pacific Ocean, killing Amelia and Fred. Others think that the plane crashed on a nearby island. Still others believe that after the Electra crashed, Amelia and Fred were captured by Japanese soldiers and treated as spies or possibly killed.

- Amelia left behind a letter explaining her love of flight. "Please know I am quite aware of the hazards. I want to do it because I want to do it. Women must try to do things as men have tried. When they fail, their failure must be but a challenge to others."

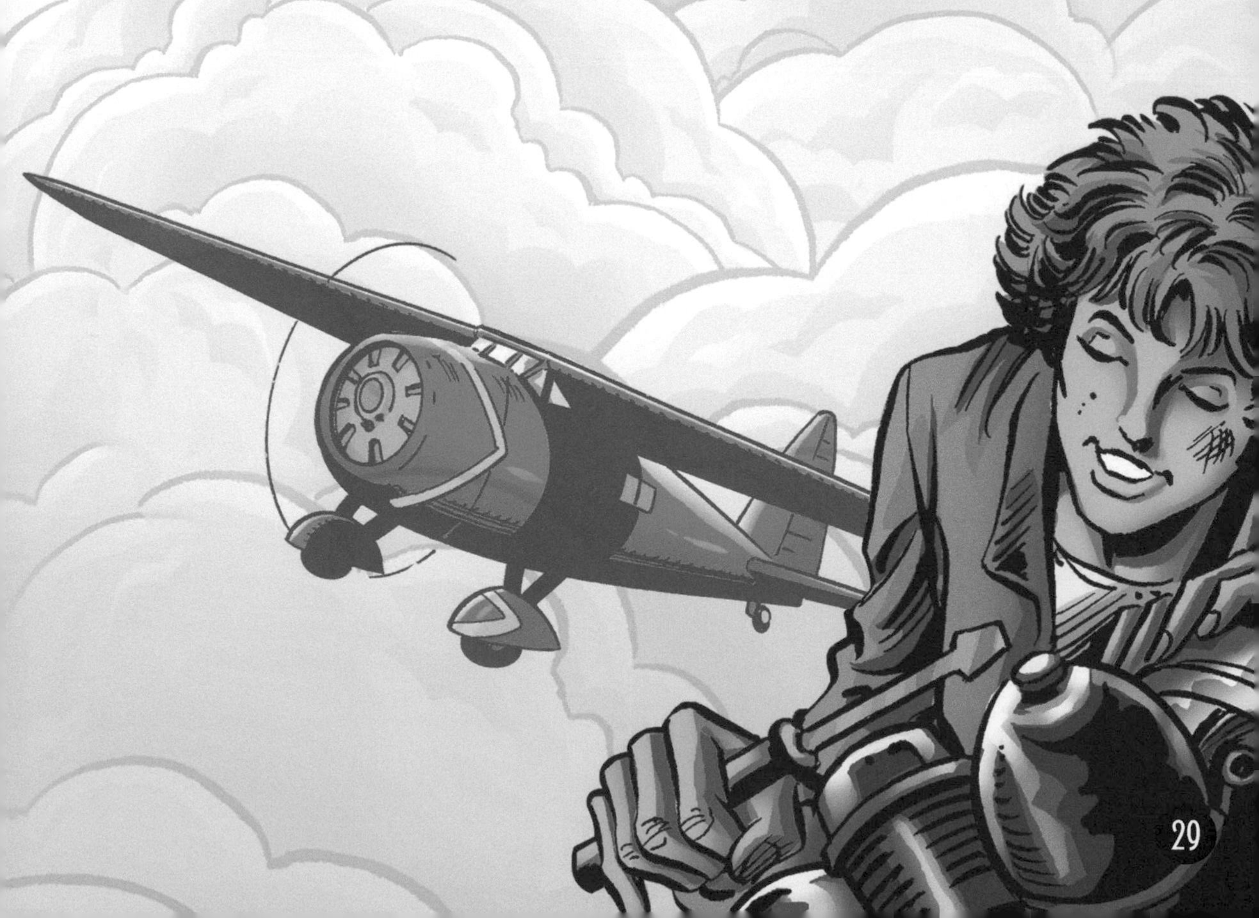

GLOSSARY

altitude (AL-ti-tood)—the height of an object above the ground

aviator (AY-vee-ay-tur)—a person who flies an airplane

bearings (BAIR-ingz)—your sense of direction in relation to where things are

gauges (GAY-jiz)—the instruments used to measure information such as speed

mechanic (muh-KAN-ik)—someone who fixes vehicles or machinery

navigator (NAV-uh-gay-tuhr)—someone who plans an airplane's flight path; navigators read maps for pilots.

INTERNET SITES

FactHound offers a safe, fun way to find Internet sites related to this book. All of the sites on FactHound have been researched by our staff.

Here's how:
1. Visit *www.facthound.com*
2. Choose your grade level.
3. Type in this book ID **0736864962** for age-appropriate sites. You may also browse subjects by clicking on letters, or by clicking on pictures and words.
4. Click on the **Fetch It** button.

FactHound will fetch the best sites for you!

READ MORE

Klingel, Cynthia Fitterer. *Amelia Earhart: Aviation Pioneer.* Our People. Chanhassen, Minn.: Child's World, 2004.

McLeese, Don. *Amelia Earhart.* Discover the Life of an American Legend. Vero Beach, Fla.: Rourke, 2002.

Micklos, John. *Unsolved: What Really Happened to Amelia Earhart?* Prime. Berkeley Heights, N.J.: Enslow, 2006.

O'Brien, Patrick. *Fantastic Flights: One Hundred Years of Flying on the Edge.* New York: Walker & Company, 2003.

BIBLIOGRAPHY

Butler, Susan. *East to the Dawn: The Life of Amelia Earhart.* Reading, Mass.: Addison-Wesley, 1997.

Earhart, Amelia. *20 hrs. 40 min.: Our Flight in the Friendship.* New York: G. P. Putnam's Sons, 1928.

Earhart, Amelia. *Last Flight.* New York: Harcourt, Brace, 1937.

Putnam, George Palmer. *Soaring Wings: A Biography of Amelia Earhart.* New York: Harcourt, Brace, and Company, 1939.

INDEX